AF204177

ABSCHLUSS-PRÜFUNGS-TRAINER

Hauptschulabschluss
Nordrhein-Westfalen

 Deine **Online-Angebote** findest du hier:

1. Melde dich auf scook.de an.
2. Gib den unten stehenden Zugangscode in die Box ein.
3. Hab viel Spaß mit den Online-Angeboten.

Dein Zugangscode auf
www.scook.de
x9abe-jonjy

Die Online-Angebote können dort
nach Bestätigung der AGB und
Lizenzbedingungen genutzt werden.

Cornelsen

Abschlussprüfungstrainer Englisch
Hauptschulabschluss | Nordrhein-Westfalen

Erarbeitet in der Redaktion von: Klaus Unger (Projektleitung); Friederike von Bülow (verantwortliche Redakteurin); sowie Cornelia Frisse, Mara Leibowitz, Paulina Schaeffer

Auf der Grundlage von Arbeitsheften folgender Autorinnen und Autoren:
Gwen Berwick, York
Sydney Thorne, York

Beratende Mitwirkung: Hartmut Bondzio, Bielefeld

Illustrationen: Cornelsen/Karen Donnelly, Brighton

Layout-Konzept: Klein&Halm Grafikdesign, Berlin

Umschlaggestaltung: Agentur Rosendahl, Berlin

Layout und technische Umsetzung: Thomas Krauß, krauß-verlagsservice, Ederheim/Hürnheim

www.cornelsen.de

Soweit in diesem Lehrwerk Personen fotografisch abgebildet sind und ihnen von der Redaktion fiktive Namen, Berufe, Dialoge und Ähnliches zugeordnet oder diese Personen in bestimmte Kontexte gesetzt werden, dienen diese Zuordnungen und Darstellungen ausschließlich der Veranschaulichung und dem besseren Verständnis des Inhalts.

1. Auflage, 1. Druck 2020

Druck: Firmengruppe APPL, aprinta Druck, Wemding

ISBN 978-3-06-034945-6

PEFC zertifiziert
Dieses Produkt stammt aus nachhaltig bewirtschafteten Wäldern und kontrollierten Quellen.
www.pefc.de
PEFC/04-32-0928

Inhaltsverzeichnis

Vorwort

Training Section

Hörverstehen – *Listening*

Leseverstehen – *Reading*

Wortschatz – *Vocabulary*

Schreiben – *Writing*

Musterprüfungen

Lösungen (als Einleger in der Mitte des Heftes)

Was erwartet dich in der Prüfung?

Liebe Schülerin, lieber Schüler,

bald ist es für dich so weit und du legst die Zentrale Prüfung (ZP 10) im Fach Englisch ab. Damit du weißt, was auf dich zukommt, wollen wir dir genau erklären, was dich in der Prüfung erwartet und wie du dich optimal vorbereiten kannst.

Die zentrale Prüfung Englisch im Überblick

Die zentrale Prüfung besteht aus zwei Teilen und dauert insgesamt 90 Minuten.

Zusätzlich erhältst du im zweiten Prüfungsteil 10 Minuten Bonuszeit, die du frei zur Orientierung oder zum Überprüfen deiner Lösungen einsetzen kannst.

	Kompetenz	Ausgangstexte und Aufgaben	Zeit	Punkte

Erster Prüfungsteil	Hörverstehen	• zwei Hörtexte
		• verschiedene Aufgabenformate:
		  – Auswahlaufgaben (*Multiple choice*)
		  – Zuordnungsaufgaben (*Matching*)
		  – Einsetzaufgaben (*Fill in the gap*)
		  – Kurzantwort-Aufgaben
		  – etc.
			20 Minuten	20 Punkte

Zweiter Prüfungsteil	Leseverstehen	• ein Lesetext
		• verschiedene Aufgabenformate:
		  – Auswahlaufgaben (*Multiple choice*), ggf. mit Begründung
		  – Richtig/Falsch-Aufgaben (*True/False*), ggf. mit Begründung
		  – Zuordnungsaufgaben (*Matching*)
		  – Einsetzaufgaben (*Fill in the gap*)
		  – Kurzantwort-Aufgaben
		  – Sequenzierungsaufgaben
		  – etc.
			70 Minuten (+ 10 Minuten Bonuszeit)	20 Punkte

	Wortschatz	• ein bis zwei Lesetexte bzw. einzelne Sätze
		• verschiedene Aufgabenformate:
		  – Auswahlaufgaben (*Multiple choice*)
		  – Zuordnungsaufgaben (*Matching*)
		  – Einsetzaufgaben (*Fill in the gap*)
		  – Ergänzungsaufgaben
		  – etc.
				15 Punkte

	Schreiben	• verschiedene Schreibformen
		  – Brief, Blogeintrag, etc.
		• verschiedene Aufgabenformate:
		  – kreatives Schreiben
		  – argumentatives Schreiben
		  – etc.
				45 Punkte

			90 Minuten (+ 10 Minuten Bonuszeit)	100 Punkte

Themen, Texte und Hilfsmittel in der Prüfung

Die Texte in der Prüfung beziehen sich auf die wichtigsten englischsprachigen Länder wie die USA, Großbritannien, Australien, Neuseeland, Kanada, Südafrika, Indien, Pakistan, Jamaika etc. In der Prüfung wird jedoch nicht dein Wissen über ein Thema oder ein Land abgefragt. Mögliche Textsorten sind z. B. Zeitungsartikel, Brief, Dialog, Interview, Touristeninformation, Präsentation, Cartoon etc.

Übrigens: Während der Prüfung sind keine Hilfsmittel erlaubt, auch **keine Wörterbücher**. In diesem Heft findest du daher auch Übungen und Tipps, die dir helfen, unbekannte Wörter und Aussagen zu entschlüsseln. Mache dir aber gleichzeitig bewusst, dass du nicht jedes einzelne Wort kennen musst, um einen Text in seinen wichtigen Aussagen zu verstehen.

Erster Prüfungsteil: Hörverstehen

Der **erste Teil des Tests** besteht aus zwei Hörtexten. Jeden Hörtext wirst du immer zweimal hören. Zwischenfragen an die Lehrkraft sind nicht erlaubt.

Es gibt unterschiedliche **Aufgabentypen**, die dir alle aus dem Englischunterricht bekannt sind:
*   **Auswahlaufgaben** (*Multiple choice*): Hier werden dir drei mögliche Lösungen angeboten, du musst die richtige Antwort ankreuzen.
*   **Zuordnungsaufgaben** (*Matching*): Bei diesen Aufgaben musst du z. B. Textstellen einer Auswahl an Aussagen, Bildern oder Personen zuordnen.
*   **Einsetzaufgaben** (*Fill in the gap*): Bei diesen Aufgaben musst du in deinen Worten Sätze vervollständigen oder Wörter in eine Lücke einsetzen.
*   **Kurzantwort-Aufgaben** (*Giving short answers*): Hier beantwortest du in deinen eigenen Worten Fragen oder gibst Beispiele aus dem Text.

Zweiter Prüfungsteil: Leseverstehen, Wortschatz und Schreiben

Der **zweite Teil des Tests** besteht aus drei Teilen:

Zunächst wird dein **Leseverstehen** abgeprüft. Die Aufgabentypen entsprechen den Aufgabentypen beim Hörverstehen. Zusätzlich gibt es folgende **Aufgabentypen**:
*   **Sequenzierungsaufgaben** (*Put in the right order*): Bei diesen Aufgaben bringst du Bilder, Aussagen, Themen etc. in die richtige Reihenfolge.
*   **Richtig/Falsch-Aufgaben** (*True/False*): Bei diesen Aufgaben musst du entscheiden, ob eine Aussage über den Text wahr oder falsch ist.

Bei manchen Aufgaben musst du eine passende Textstelle heraussuchen und zitieren, um deine Lösung zu begründen.

Anschließend werden deine **Wortschatzkenntnisse** durch folgende Aufgabentypen abgeprüft:
*   **Auswahlaufgaben** (*Multiple choice*): Hier erhältst du z. B. eine Auswahl an Begriffen und musst dich für den richtigen Begriff entscheiden.
*   Bei **Zuordnungsaufgaben** (*Matching*) musst du z. B. Umschreibungen oder Begriffe mit gleicher oder gegensätzlicher Bedeutung zuordnen.
*   **Einsetzaufgaben** (*Fill in the gap*): Bei diesem Aufgabenformat setzt du in einen Text passende Wörter oder Begriffe ein.
*   Bei **Ergänzungsaufgaben** musst du z. B. Wörter zu einem vorgegebenen Thema ergänzen (z. B. in Form einer *mind map*).

Im Prüfungsteil **Schreiben** musst selbst einen kurzen Text (ca. 120 Wörter) verfassen. Meistens wird ein Text (z. B. eine Stellenanzeige oder ein Brief) vorgegeben, auf den du schriftlich reagieren musst. Hierbei werden z. B. **beschreibende, berichtende oder argumentierende Texte** (wie Bildbeschreibung, Erlebnisbericht oder eine kurze Meinungsäußerung) von dir verlangt. Meistens musst du diese Texte in Form z. B. eines **Briefs** oder einer **E-Mail**, eines **(Zeitungs-)Artikels** oder eines **Blogeintrags** verfassen.

Wie arbeitest du mit diesem Heft?

In diesem Heft lernst du durch gezielte Übungen, wie du die Aufgaben zu allen Prüfungsteilen bearbeiten kannst. Darüber hinaus bekommst du konkrete Prüfungsbeispiele. Das Heft ist deshalb wie folgt aufgebaut:

Das **erste Kapitel**, die *Training Section*, gliedert sich in die vier Kompetenzbereiche, die in der zentralen Prüfung abgeprüft werden: **Hörverstehen**, **Leseverstehen**, **Wortschatz** und **Schreiben**.

Die *Training Section* enthält:

- Hinweise zum Ablauf und zur Bewertung jedes einzelnen Kompetenzbereichs
- Beispiele und Tipps für alle Aufgabenformate, die in der Prüfung vorkommen können, also *Multiple choice*, *True/False* etc.
- zahlreiche Strategien zum Umgang mit typischen Schwierigkeiten, wie z.B. Verständnisproblemen
- vielfältige Aufgaben zum Üben aller Kompetenzbereiche (*Now you*).

> **Tipp**
>
> Blau umrandete Felder markieren Tipps, die dir bei den Aufgaben helfen.

Es empfiehlt sich, die *Training Section* als Erstes durchzuarbeiten, und zwar Kompetenzbereich für Kompetenzbereich. So verschaffst du dir einen Überblick darüber, was du schon gut kannst, wo du noch üben solltest und welche Strategien dir dabei helfen.

Das **zweite Kapitel** bietet dir drei komplette **Musterprüfungen**, die jeweils alle vier Kompetenzbereiche (Hörverstehen, Leseverstehen, Wortschatz, Schreiben) enthalten. Sie sind den Prüfungen der letzten Jahre nachempfunden. Du lernst dadurch Schritt für Schritt die gesamte Prüfungssituation und den Aufbau einer Prüfung kennen.

Wenn du feststellst, dass du mit einem Kompetenzbereich oder einem Aufgabenformat noch Schwierigkeiten hast, gehe zurück in die *Training Section*. Wiederhole dort gezielt die entsprechenden Übungen und Strategien. Du kannst auch die Online-Übungen zu Grammatik und Wortschatz auf www.scook.de nutzen.

Die **Tonaufnahmen und Hörtexte** für die *Training Section* und die Musterprüfungen findest du ebenfalls online unter www.scook.de. Das Kopfhörer-Symbol mit Track-Nummer im Heft zeigt dir an, welchen Hörtext du für die Aufgabe anhören musst.

Mit dem **Lösungsteil** in der Mitte des Heftes kannst du deine Ergebnisse überprüfen und – wenn nötig – verbessern.

Nützliche Tipps zur Prüfungsvorbereitung erhältst du auf S. 40.

Nun kannst du zuversichtlich sein, dass du weißt, was in der Zentralen Prüfung 10 (ZP 10) auf dich zukommt, und dass du die unterschiedlichen Aufgabenstellungen geübt hast und kennst.

> Zusätzlich kannst du dein Grundwissen in den Bereichen Grammatik und Wortschatz mithilfe von Online-Übungen wiederholen und vertiefen. Nutze dazu den Zugangscode auf Seite 1 (www.scook.de).
>
> Ebenfalls findest du die Tonaufnahmen zu den Höraufgaben als MP3-Downloads und die Hörtexte. Nutze dazu ebenfalls den Code von Seite 1.

Viel Spaß beim Training mit diesem Heft und viel Erfolg bei der Prüfung!

ABSCHLUSS-PRÜFUNGS-TRAINER

Nordrhein-Westfalen

Training Section

Hörverstehen – *Listening*

1. Ablauf und Bewertung der Prüfung

Erster Prüfungsteil

Im **ersten Prüfungsteil** geht es um das **Hörverstehen**. Du hast für diesen Teil maximal 20 Minuten Zeit, in denen du zwei Hörtexte bearbeiten musst.

Wenn du mit dem ersten Prüfungsteil (Hörverstehen) fertig bist, musst du deine Prüfungsunterlagen für diesen Teil abgeben. Achte also darauf, dass du alle Aufgaben bearbeitet und deine Antworten noch einmal kontrolliert hast. Nachdem du abgegeben hast, kannst du deine Antworten nicht mehr korrigieren.

Ablauf beim Hörverstehen

Beim **Hörverstehen** hast du zunächst eine Minute Zeit, um die Aufgaben zu lesen. Nutze diese Gelegenheit zur Orientierung: Was verlangen die Aufgaben von dir? Worauf musst du beim Zuhören achten? Dann hörst du den Hörtext zum ersten Mal und bearbeitest dabei die Aufgaben. Abschließend hörst du den Hörtext noch ein zweites Mal.

Bewertung beim Hörverstehen

Ein Wörterbuch ist in der gesamten Zentralen Prüfung 10 (ZP10) nicht erlaubt. Du musst aber keine Angst vor Grammatik- oder Rechtschreibfehlern in deinen Antworten haben. Solange man versteht, was du geschrieben hast, gehen sie **in diesem Prüfungsteil** nicht in die Bewertung ein.

Das Hörverstehen macht 20 % deiner Gesamtnote aus.

2. Typische Aufgabenformate in NRW

In diesem Kapitel lernst du typische Aufgabenformate zum Hörverstehen in der Zentralen Prüfung 10 (ZP10) kennen. Du hörst ein Radio-Interview über die kanadische Stadt Calgary.
Die Tipp-Kästen enthalten Hilfen, wie du mit Schwierigkeiten umgehen kannst.

Calgary's skyways

You are going to hear a radio interview about the Skyway network in Calgary, a city in western Canada.

Auswahlaufgaben *(Multiple choice)*

> • *First read the task.*
> • *Then listen to the first part of the interview.*
> • *While you are listening, tick the correct box.*
> • *At the end you will hear the interview again.*

The underground cities in Canada …

a) ☐ are famous tourist sites.

b) ☐ are useless when it's cold.

c) ☐ help people to stay warm in cold weather.

Tipp

Bei *Multiple choice*-Aufgaben werden einzelne Wörter aus dem Hörtext häufig ersetzt durch:

ähnliche Begriffe:
climate/winter　　　　=　cold *weather* in
im Hörtext　　　　　　　Antwort c)

Gegensätze:
useful　　　　　　　　≠　*useless*
im Hörtext　　　　　　　in Antwort b)

Antwort c) könnte also die richtige sein.

Zuordnungsaufgabe *(Matching)*

- *First read the task.*
- *Then listen to the second part of the interview.*
- *Match the place names (1–5) with the pictures (A–E).*
- *At the end you will hear the interview again.*

Tipp

- Musst du Bilder zuordnen, so überlege, wie das Dargestellte auf Englisch heißen könnte. Bild B zeigt hier z. B. ein Freiluft-Kino. Achte im Hörtext also auf Begriffe wie *movie, watch, cinema, open air* oder *theatre*.
- Achtung! Die Ortsnamen können im Hörtext in einer anderen Reihenfolge vorkommen.

1 Burlington: _____   **2** Stoney Creek: _____   **3** Kissimmee: _____

4 Jacksonville: _____   **5** Jasper National Park: _____

Einsetzaufgaben *(Fill in the gap)*

- *First read the tasks 1–2.*
- *Then listen to the third part of the interview.*
- *While you are listening, fill in the gaps.*
- *At the end you will hear the interview again.*

Overhead pedestrian passage in Calgary

1 Calgary has a system of _____ passageways 15 feet up in the air.

2 There are passageways between _____ all over downtown Calgary.

Tipp

Denke an den Sinn der fehlenden Wörter.

1 Die *passageways* sind in der Luft, **über** deinem **Kopf** …

2 Die *passageways* sind *downtown*, also in der Innenstadt, wo sehr viele **Gebäude** stehen …

Kurzantwort-Aufgaben *(Giving short answers)*

4

- *First read the tasks 1–2.*
- *Then listen to the fourth part of the interview and answer the questions.*
- *At the end you will hear the interview again.*

1 What are **two** advantages for pedestrians?

a) _____

b) _____

2 Why do some people criticize the skyways?

_____

> **Tipp**
> - Bei diesem Aufgabentyp sollst du die Antworten in deinen eigenen Worten geben. Du brauchst nicht Wort für Wort aus dem Hörtext zu zitieren.
> - Fragen mit zwei Teilen – a) und b) – sind zwei Punkte wert. Gib also zwei verschiedene Antworten.

3. Umgang mit Verständnisproblemen

Die Hörtexte in der Zentralen Prüfung 10 (ZP 10) enthalten manchmal Wörter, die du vielleicht nicht kennst oder die du auch beim zweiten Hören nicht verstehst. Keine Panik – das ist ganz normal! In diesem Kapitel lernst du Strategien kennen, die dir helfen, die wesentlichen Inhalte trotzdem zu erfassen und die Aufgabe zu lösen. Du hörst dafür einen Werbefilm über die Niagarafälle zunächst mit Störgeräuschen.

The Niagara Falls

The following text is the audio track of a publicity film about the Niagara Falls.

5

- *First read the tasks 1–5.*
- *Then listen to the programme. You can read the text (p. 12) while you are listening.*
- *Do tasks 1–5: tick the correct box or fill in the information.*
- *At the end you will hear the text again (task 6).*

1 The Horseshoe Falls ...

a) ☐ are smaller than the American falls.

b) ☐ are fully in Canada.

c) ☐ are for the most part in Canada.

> **Tipp**
> Wende bei kniffligen Aufgaben das **Ausschlussverfahren** an:
> - Markiere die Stelle im ersten Absatz, die Antwort a) ausschließt.
> - Zwischen b) und c) kannst du dich noch nicht entscheiden: Im Hörtext könnte es nämlich heißen *only in Canada*, **mainly in Canada**, **partly in Canada** oder **fully in Canada**.
>
> Beim zweiten Hören kannst du jetzt gezielt zwischen zwei möglichen Antworten entscheiden – das ist leichter als zwischen dreien.

2 The people on the boat tours need protection. Give **one** example of how they protect themselves.

_____

> **Tipp**
> Hier kannst du dir helfen, indem du **Vermutungen** anstellst:
> - Die Touristen sind laut Hörtext *wet* (= nass).
> - Wie kann man sich gegen Nässe schützen? Zu erwarten sind also Wörter wie *raincoat, umbrella, waterproof* etc.
>
> Achte beim zweiten Zuhören besonders gut auf diese Stelle. Mit dieser Vorbereitung wirst du sie bestimmt besser verstehen.

3 The land on the American side of the falls ...

a) ☐ can only be reached if you pay.

b) ☐ was the first state park in the USA.

c) ☐ looks like Central Park in New York City.

> **Tipp**
>
> Wende das Ausschlussverfahren an!
> Lösung c) kannst du sogar, wenn du fast nichts verstanden hast, mit dem gesunden Menschenverstand ausschließen. Warum?
>
> Lösung a) kannst du ebenfalls ausschließen, wenn du die relevante Stelle im Text verstanden hast. Markiere diese Stelle im Hörtext (S. 12).

4 Annie Taylor went over the falls in a barrel

because _____.

> **Tipp**
>
> Was erfährst du im Hörtext über Annie Taylor? Kannst du daraus schließen, zu welchem Zweck sie so etwas Gefährliches getan hat?

5 When Annie Taylor's friends opened the barrel, they found that she was ...

a) ☐ dead.

b) ☐ injured.

c) ☐ unhurt.

> **Tipp**
>
> • Markiere im Hörtext (S. 12) das Wort, mit dem du Lösung a) ausschließen kannst.
> • Das Wort *although* (= obwohl) im Text leitet einen Gegensatz ein: Obwohl sie nichts gebrochen hatte, war sie _____.
> Dank dieses Wortes kannst du also beim zweiten Hören zwischen Lösung b) und Lösung c) wählen. Siehst du wie?

> • *Now read tasks 6 and 7.*
> • *Then listen to the programme again. This time it's complete.*
> • *Do task 6 while you are listening.*
> • *Then do task 7 (p. 12).*

6 Listen to the complete programme. Note the exact words in the recording.

a) ... the Horseshoe Falls are the biggest and they're _____ in Canada.

b) ... everyone here is wearing _____.

c) ... these falls on the American side are actually part of _____ state park.

d) Annie (...) decided to go over the falls to _____.

e) But although Annie (amazingly!) came out with no broken bones, she _____

_____ – it was bleeding.

Tipp

Die Tonaufnahme (Track 5) enthält Störgeräusche, die einige Textstellen unverständlich machen. Im folgenden Hörtext sind diese Stellen durch Schwärzungen markiert. Dieses Vorgehen soll dir zeigen, dass du einige der Aufgaben 1–5 trotz der fehlenden Textstellen lösen kannst. Bei anderen Aufgaben kannst du mithilfe der Tipps zumindest Vermutungen anstellen.

Beim zweiten Hören (Track 6) in Aufgabe 6 hörst du den Text ohne Störgeräusche. Nun kannst du überprüfen, ob deine Vermutungen richtig waren.

Welcome to the Niagara Falls! These astonishing natural waterfalls are on the border between the USA and Canada. They consist of three waterfalls. The two smaller ones are in the USA. But these amazing falls, called the Horseshoe Falls, are the biggest and they're ▮▮▮ in Canada. The Niagara Falls are located near important urban centres. It only takes half an hour by car to get to Buffalo.

These tourists have just landed at Buffalo International Airport and they're on their way to see the famous falls. In fact, about 30 million people visit the Niagara Falls each year! This group is going on the very popular Maid of the Mist tour – a boat tour to the bottom of the waterfalls. The air here is full of ▮▮▮ ▮▮▮ – that's why everyone here is wearing ▮▮▮. But don't be fooled – most of them are going to get wet anyway. Oh! Here comes the next shower!

Accessing the falls is easy. That's great because it means that thousands of people can come and see the fantastic sight. But it also means that the falls have to be well protected and taken care of. In fact, these falls on the American side are actually part of ▮▮▮ ▮▮▮ state park. It was designed by the same man who laid out this well-known park. Do you recognize it? It's Central Park in New York City. Luckily state parks don't charge entrance – so you don't have to pay to see the falls. Tourists can stand right next to the top of the Horseshoe Falls and watch the water spilling over. Isn't it amazing?

Sometimes people have gone over the falls. Some have even done it by choice. This is Annie Taylor – she was the first person to ride over the Niagara Falls, way back in 1901, on her 63rd birthday. After her husband and son had died, Annie was facing poverty and decided to go over the falls ▮▮▮. And guess what she used to cross the falls: this thing. That's right – a wooden barrel. The sort of barrel that was used to store wine or beer. Crazy, isn't it? She put cushions and a mattress inside and asked some friends to push the barrel in the right direction at the top – and other friends to open it when she got to the bottom of the falls. And she did: she went over the top of the falls, the barrel fell, and when her friends opened it, she was alive.

But although Annie (amazingly!) came out with no broken bones, she ▮▮▮: it was bleeding. After her crazy experiment, Annie warned other people against doing the same thing. We'll take your advice, Annie.

7 Now use your information from task 6 to check your answers to tasks 1–5.

4. Hörverstehen – *Now you*

In diesem Kapitel kannst du die Strategien, die du auf den letzten Seiten kennengelernt hast, bei ausgewählten Aufgaben zum Hörverstehen gezielt üben. Dafür hörst du ein Telefongespräch über ein Radrennen in Yorkshire und ein Radio-Interview über die jamaikanische Reggae-Legende Bob Marley.

The Tour de Yorkshire

Sarah from Ireland and Mo from Yorkshire are talking about a cycling race in Yorkshire. You will hear their telephone conversation.

Yellow bicycle on the city walls of York, 2014

Auswahlaufgaben *(Multiple choice)*

7

> * *First read the tasks 1–5.*
> * *Then listen to the dialogue.*
> * *While you are listening, tick the correct box.*
> * *At the end you will hear the dialogue again.*
> * *Now read the tasks. You have <u>one minute</u> to do this.*

> * *Now listen to the dialogue and do the tasks.*

1 In 2014 the Tour de France cycling race …

   a) ☐ began in France and came to Yorkshire.

   b) ☐ went through other countries and then came to Yorkshire.

   c) ☐ began in Yorkshire.

2 During the Tour de Yorkshire race …

   a) ☐ cycling fans rode yellow bicycles.

   b) ☐ people bought lots of yellow bicycles.

   c) ☐ there were old yellow bicycles on the sides of the roads.

3 The organizers of the Tour de France …

   a) ☐ planned for large crowds.

   b) ☐ didn't expect the positive reaction from people in Yorkshire.

   c) ☐ hoped that many people would join the cyclists.

4 The Tour de France …

   a) ☐ was in Yorkshire for 21 days.

   b) ☐ made people in Yorkshire want to see more cycling races.

   c) ☐ went from Yorkshire directly on to France.

5 The Tour de Yorkshire cycling race …

   a) ☐ includes hills that are difficult even for experienced cyclists.

   b) ☐ uses wide roads where cycling is very easy.

   c) ☐ has become a very popular off-road race.

Bob Marley

Radio presenter Joshua Needham is talking to Reggae expert Gwen Devlin about the Jamaican singer-songwriter Bob Marley.

Gemischte Aufgabenformate *(Mixed tasks)*

> • *First read the tasks 1–4.*
> • *Then listen to the interview.*
> • *While you are listening, tick the correct box, match the sentence halves or answer the questions.*
> • *At the end you will hear the interview again.*
> • *Now read the tasks. You have <u>one minute</u> to do this.*

> • *Now listen to the interview and do the tasks.*

Bob Marley (1945–1981)

1 Match the people (1–3) with the sentence halves (A–D).
You will <u>not need one</u> of the sentence halves.

1 Bob Marley …	**A** used to live in Sussex, England.
2 Bob Marley's father …	**B** saw his father very often.
3 Bob Marley's mother …	**C** was born in February 1945.
	D was 18 when Bob was born.

2 Bob Marley's first band was called "The _____".

3 Bob Marley's early song *Simmer Down* was a success in Jamaica. Which fact proves this?

_____

4 Bob Marley was seen as a controversial figure because …

a) ☐ he wasn't involved in politics.

b) ☐ he smoked cannabis and was politically active.

c) ☐ he didn't like Africa.

Leseverstehen – *Reading*

1. Ablauf und Bewertung der Prüfung

Zweiter Prüfungsteil

Das **Leseverstehen** gehört – zusammen mit dem Wortschatz und dem Schreiben – zum **zweiten Prüfungsteil**, für den du insgesamt 70 Minuten zur Verfügung hast. Zusätzlich hast du zehn Minuten Bonuszeit, die du nutzen kannst, wenn du mehr Zeit benötigst.
Verschaffe dir zu Beginn des zweiten Teils einen Überblick über alle Aufgaben, die du in diesen 70 Minuten bearbeiten sollst. Du kannst selbst entscheiden, mit welchem Teil du anfängst.

Ablauf beim Leseverstehen

In diesem Teil der Prüfung liest du einen Text. Dann bearbeitest du Aufgaben zu diesem Text.

Bewertung beim Leseverstehen

Auch beim Leseverstehen sind Wörterbücher nicht erlaubt. Bei deinen Antworten werden Rechtschreib- und Grammatikfehler nur dann bewertet, wenn man nicht mehr verstehen kann, was du geschrieben hast. Das Leseverstehen macht 20 % deiner Gesamtnote aus.

2. Typische Aufgabenformate in NRW

Im Folgenden lernst du typische Textsorten und Aufgabentypen kennen, die dich bei der Zentralen Prüfung 10 (ZP 10) im Bereich Leseverstehen erwarten können. Die Aufgaben beziehen sich auf einen Sachtext (*Australia's Stolen Generations*), einen fiktionalen Text (*Kasun*) und einen Comic. Die Tipp-Kästen enthalten nützliche Strategien, um mit typischen Schwierigkeiten umzugehen.

Australia's Stolen Generation

The following texts are from a museum about Aboriginal people in Australia.

Auswahlaufgaben mit Begründung
(Multiple choice – with evidence from the text)

- *First read the text.*
- *Then tick the correct box.*

In the mid-20th century the Australian government made a new rule that allowed officials to take Aboriginal children away from their mothers and fathers – even if
5 the parents wanted to keep their children at home.
Over 250,000 Aboriginal children had to leave their homes but some say it was as many as 500,000.

Tipp

In *Multiple choice*-Aufgaben werden einzelne Wörter aus dem Lesetext oft ersetzt durch:
- Wörter mit einer **gleichen oder ähnlichen Bedeutung**, wie *pretty – beautiful*
- Wörter mit einer **gegensätzlichen Bedeutung**, wie *pretty – ugly*

Das kann dir helfen, die richtige Lösung zu finden:
- Zu *die* und *illness* in Lösung a) gibt es im Text keine Wörter mit gleicher oder gegensätzlicher Bedeutung. Lösung a) ist also falsch.
- Zu *stolen* und *parents* in Lösung b) gibt es im Text Wörter mit gleicher Bedeutung, nämlich _____ und _____. Lösung b) könnte also die richtige Lösung sein.
- Zu *stay* in Lösung c) gibt es im Text einen Gegensatz, nämlich _____. Lösung c) ist daher wahrscheinlich auch falsch.

Thousands of Aboriginal Australian children ...

a) ☐ died of an illness.

b) ☐ were stolen from their parents.

c) ☐ were forced to stay with their parents.

One piece of evidence from the text:

_____

Tipp

Wenn du deine Antwort mit einem Zitat belegen sollst, kannst du die entsprechende Textstelle einfach abschreiben.

Denk an die richtige Zeichensetzung bei Zitaten und vergiss nicht, die richtigen Zeilen anzugeben:

z. B. "[...] *to take Aboriginal children away from their mothers and fathers*" (ll. 3–4) oder "[...] *had to leave their homes*" (ll. 7–8)

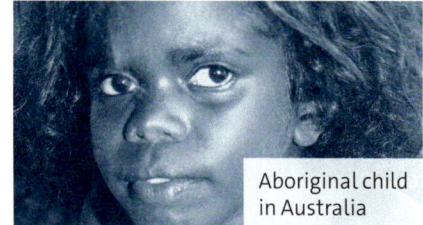

Aboriginal child in Australia

Einsetzaufgaben *(Fill in the gap)*

- *First read the text.*
- *Then complete the sentences.*

> The Aboriginal children were brought to new English-speaking families where they were not allowed to speak their own language. And they were given the typical
> 5 foods of white Australians, even though they weren't used to it.

Tipp

Manchmal musst du die Informationen aus dem Text umformulieren:

im Text:	deine Antwort:
The children (...) were <u>not allowed</u> to speak their own language.	... they <u>had to</u> speak _____.

When the Aboriginal children came to their new homes, they had to speak _____ .

Richtig/Falsch-Aufgaben mit Begründung *(True/False – with evidence from the text)*

- *First read the text.*
- *Then tick the correct box and give evidence.*

> The parents were not told where their children were. The children were not allowed to have any contact with their parents. The result was that all contact
> 5 with their families, their language, their music and their way of life was broken off.

A lot of Aboriginal Australians lost connection with their culture.

This statement is ...

☐ true.   ☐ false.

One piece of evidence from the text:

_____

Tipp

Wichtig:
- Steht in der Aufgabenstellung *Give evidence from the text*, so musst du wörtlich aus dem Text zitieren.
- Steht in der Aufgabenstellung *You <u>can</u> quote from the text*, so kannst du wörtlich aus dem Text zitieren <u>oder</u> deine Antwort frei formulieren.

Tipp

Achte auf Sammelbegriffe, die für eine Reihe von Beispielen stehen können:

im Text:	in der Aufgabe:
families, language, music, way of life	Sammelbegriff: _____

Kasun

The following text is from a story about Kasun, a boy who lives in Sri Lanka.
In this text, Kasun writes about his first day at a new school.

Zuordnungsaufgaben *(Matching)*

On the first day at my new school in Colombo I was scared stiff. Not that I showed it, of course. I acted relaxed while the whole time, my knees were like jelly.

5 My mum seemed to be calm, but I knew her better than that. Her red eyes told their own story.

When I got to school, all the other kids in Grade 9 seemed to know each other. Maybe because they all lived in Colombo.

10 Even the teachers had the same accent as the other students did. But I was from Kuruwita, a smaller town outside the capital, and I felt like a fish out of water.

- *First read the text.*
- *Then match the beginnings of sentences (1–3) with the endings (A–D). You will <u>not need one</u> ending.*

---

1 Before going to school Kasun acted …	**A**	as if he was calm.
2 On his first day of school Kasun felt …	**B**	was frightened.
3 The other kids at school …	**C**	were from a different city than Kasun.
	D	like he didn't belong there.

Tipp

Es ist nicht wichtig, für welchen Satzanfang du zuerst das passende Ende findest.
Lies dir zunächst alle Satzteile aufmerksam durch. Du musst nicht mit dem ersten Satzanfang beginnen.
Vielleicht fällt es dir beim dritten Satzanfang leichter, das passende Ende zu finden.

- *Read the text again.*
- *Then match each of the expressions from the text (1–3) with <u>one</u> of the feelings (A–D). You will <u>not need one</u> feeling.*

1 "I was scared stiff."	**A**	nervous
2 "My knees were like jelly."	**B**	uncomfortable
3 "I felt like a fish out of water."	**C**	frightened
	D	bored

Tipp

Versuche, die Bedeutung einer ganzen Formulierung zu verstehen statt der einzelnen Wörter.

Beispiel:

I felt like a fish out of water.

Kasun fühlte sich nicht plötzlich wie ein Fisch!

fish out of water ist ein Bild dafür, dass er sich

_____ fühlte.

Kurzantwort-Aufgaben *(Giving short answers)*

"Hey, what's your name?"
I turned around and saw a big boy. He was smiling. But was he talking to me? Or to somebody behind me? I was too scared to answer.
5 "Hey, what's the problem?" said the boy, and took a step closer to me. I could only look at his big hands. Was he going to hit me?

"Do you think I'm going to bite you? Hi. I'm Sahan." he said.
"I ... I'm Kasun," I stuttered. "I'm not from 10 Colombo. I'm from Kuruwita, but I ..."
"Hey, calm down, you're talking too fast," laughed Sahan.

- *Now read a second extract from* Kasun.
- *Then answer the questions 1–3.*

1 Why doesn't Kasun answer the big boy's first question?

_____

2 What does Kasun think when the big boy comes nearer?

_____

3 How do we know that Kasun is very nervous?

_____

Tipp

Gib bei Kurzantwort-Aufgaben deine Antwort in deinen eigenen Worten – dafür bekommst du mehr Punkte! Du brauchst nicht Wort für Wort aus dem Lesetext zu zitieren. Es kann aber helfen, die relevante Stelle im Text zu markieren.

Cartoon strip

This is a cartoon strip from a youth magazine.

Sequenzierungsaufgaben *(Put in the right order)*

Tipp

Bei dieser Art Aufgabe ist es wichtig, zunächst den Anfang des Textes zu finden.

Hier: *it* im ersten Satz von **B** *(He doesn't know about it.)* bezieht sich auf etwas, das schon gesagt wurde. Also kann **B** nicht das erste Bild sein.

Achte auch auf die Bilder: Die Personen sprechen abwechselnd. Dies kann dir helfen, die Reihenfolge zu bestimmen.

A — Oh, I'm really sorry. Poor Mark must be so sad.

C — I have bad news. I've broken off my relationship with Mark.

B — He doesn't know about it. I haven't told him yet.

- *Look at the three pictures from a cartoon strip and read the speech bubbles.*
- *Put the pictures (A–C) in the right order.*

Picture 1: _____   Picture 2: _____   Picture 3: _____

3. Umgang mit Verständnisproblemen

In der Zentralen Prüfung 10 (ZP 10) ist kein Wörterbuch erlaubt. Die Texte zum Leseverstehen können aber manchmal Wörter enthalten, die du nicht kennst. Doch keine Angst!
Mit den richtigen Strategien kannst du die Aufgaben oft trotzdem richtig lösen.
• Markiere unbekannte Wörter.
• Versuche, dir die Wörter z. B. aus dem Zusammenhang zu erschließen.
• Bei einigen Aufgaben musst du nicht jedes Wort im Text verstehen. Es reicht, wenn du die allgemeine Aussage verstehst.

Dieses Kapitel präsentiert einige wichtige Strategien anhand eines Sachtextes über die Everglades.

The Everglades

This text is about the Everglades – a region of tropical wetlands in Florida – and the problems about roadworks there.

• *Read the text.*
• *Then do the tasks 1–4.*

> Neu – kannst du den Sinn aus bekannten Wörtern erschließen? Vielleicht ist es aber für deine Antwort auch unwichtig!

> Vielleicht neu – aber du kannst es aus dem Zusammenhang erschließen: Umwelt/Lebensraum der Alligatoren ist in Gefahr.

1 The wetlands of the Everglades in the south of the state of Florida are famous for their alligators, snakes, turtles and other wildlife. Sometimes, tourists can see them from airboats or on specially-provided hiking trails. Visitor centres show alligators feeding and inform tourists about how the alligators' environment is endangered.

> Neu – aber aus dem Zusammenhang kannst du schließen: Die Haustiere sind in den Everglades, weil die Menschen sie herausgelassen haben.

> Neu – aber du kennst *danger* = Gefahr.

2 In fact, the Everglades are facing huge environmental problems. Its lakes and rivers are polluted by dirty waste water from the city of Miami. And pets released into the Everglades by people from the city have also become a danger to the original wildlife.
But the biggest headache of all is that the wetlands are drying out. This is partly because the slow-flowing Kissimmee River was replaced by a completely straight canal in the 1960s. It lets the water flow away too quickly. And what makes it worse is the U.S. Highway 41, which was completed in 1928. It cuts through 275 miles of the Everglades on a big wall of earth. This prevents water from flowing into the southern part of the Everglades.

> Neues Verb – aber du kennst *dry* = trocken

> Du kennst *wet* und *land*. Was könnten also *wetlands* sein?

> Neu – aber aus dem Zusammenhang kannst du schließen: Dieser Erdwall hindert das Wasser am Fließen.

3 The plan is to fill parts of the canal to let the water to flow into the slower river. A new bridge will be built for cars on to allow water to pass under it.

1 Match the paragraphs (1–4) with the topics (A–D).
There is <u>one more topic</u> than you need.

paragraph 1	**A** Educating the public
paragraph 2	**B** What is being done to help
paragraph 3	**C** The beauty of the Everglades
	D Pollution and shortness of water

> **Tipp**
>
> Bei solchen Aufgaben geht es darum, dass du den Text im Großen und Ganzen verstehst, selbst wenn du nicht jedes Wort kennst.
>
> Hier kannst du z. B. *topic D* zuordnen, selbst wenn du *pollution* nicht kennst:
>
> 1. In zwei Absätzen geht es um Wasser.
> 2. Zu einem dieser beiden Absätze passt auch ein anderes *topic*, nämlich _____ . So grenzt du die Auswahl ein.
>
> Also gehört *topic D* wahrscheinlich zu *paragraph* _____.

2 What do visitors do in the visitor centres?
Give **two** examples.

> **Tipp**
>
> Hier musst du das, was im Text steht, nur leicht umformulieren, damit es zum vorgegebenen Satzanfang passt.

a) They _____ .

b) They _____ .

3 How do the people of Miami create problems for wildlife in the Everglades?

a) They _____ .

b) They _____ .

> **Tipp**
>
> Auch hier musst du die Informationen im Text umformulieren.
> Im Text steht „[...] *lakes and rivers are polluted by dirty waste water from the city of Miami.*"
>
> Die Antwort für **a)** muss also lauten *They pollute* _____ .

4 **Highway 41**

Now complete the following sentences:

a) The government wants to _____ .

b) This will be better because _____ .

> **Tipp**
>
> Die Regierung möchte Teile des Kanals wieder auffüllen – das stimmt, ist aber hier trotzdem nicht die richtige Antwort! Warum nicht?
>
> Schau noch mal auf die Überschrift zu Aufgabe **4**. Worum muss es bei den Teilaufgaben **a)** und **b)** also gehen?
>
> → Lies immer Titel und Arbeitsanweisung genau!

4. Leseverstehen – *Now you*

In diesem Kapitel kannst du die Strategien, die du auf den letzten Seiten kennen gelernt hast, gezielt üben. Dafür liest du einen Artikel über die Filmindustrie in Neuseeland, einen Blog über ein Motorrad-Rennen und einen Zeitungsartikel über indische Küche in Großbritannien.

Filming in New Zealand

This text is taken from an article in a film magazine.

Mount Ngauruhoe

Auswahlaufgaben *(Multiple choice)*

New Zealand's amazing nature has long attracted the world's top film directors.

The three *Lord of the Rings* films, for example, were filmed in different areas of
5　New Zealand, even in some of the country's national parks. The films were also shot on spectacular mountains such as Mount Ngauruhoe, a treeless live volcano, and along rivers, lakes and wild canyons. Some scenes
10　were filmed in the soft green hills near Matamata as well.

One of the advantages of filming in New Zealand is the small number of people living there: only four and a half million people in a
15　country about the same size as the United Kingdom (population: 64 million). So there are fewer buildings to ruin the views of open countryside.

However, New Zealand's cities have also appeared in films. In the film *King Kong*, for
20　example, many of the scenes that should look like they are set in New York were actually filmed in Wellington. It's New Zealand's capital, though not its largest city. Wellington is also the southernmost capital city in the world.
25　Still, the city has a growing film industry and professional experience of working with some famous film directors.

> • *First read the text.*
> • *Then do the tasks 1–4. Tick the correct box.*

1 The *Lord of the Rings* trilogy was filmed in …

　a) ☐ more than one region in New Zealand.

　b) ☐ national parks only.

　c) ☐ only one part of New Zealand.

2 Scenes from Lord of the Rings were filmed …

　a) ☐ in wild hills near Matamata.

　b) ☐ in very different areas.

　c) ☐ on a volcano famous for its trees.

3 New Zealand …

　a) ☐ is as big as the United Kingdom.

　b) ☐ has a population the same size as the United Kingdom.

　c) ☐ has a bigger population than the United Kingdom.

4 Wellington …

　a) ☐ is New Zealand's biggest city.

　b) ☐ looks a little bit like New York.

　c) ☐ has good scenery but no local film industry.

The Isle of Man TT race

The Isle of Man is a small island between Britain and Ireland. It is famous for its motorcycle racing. This text is from a blog written by a person living on the Isle of Man.

Richtig/Falsch-Aufgaben mit Begründung *(True/False – with reasons)*

I live on one of Europe's quietest islands – the Isle of Man. It is set in the Irish Sea about half way between England and Ireland. We have beautiful unspoilt countryside and narrow
5 country roads. And every May or June we have the TT (Tourist Trophy) race. It's one of the most famous motorcycle racing events in the world. The amazing thing is that it takes place on about 50 kilometres of our narrow public roads.
10 Every year the roads are closed to the public for a week of practice runs and a week of racing. That means two weeks of road chaos on the island, when it's hard for locals to get from one part of the island to another. A trip that usually
15 takes ten minutes can take half an hour or more.
The only way you can bring your motorbike is by ferry. In 2015 about 36,0000 fans travelled to the Isle of Man. They brought over 14,000 motorbikes with them. That is 17 % more than
20 the year before.
The TT has run every year since 1907. But there were no races during the First and Second World Wars. The TT race has not always been popular with racers, however. Between 1907 and
25 2015 no less than 246 people have lost their lives during the event – 141 racers, and 105 spectators and other members of the public. As a result,

Tourist Trophy race, Isle of Man (2015)

the event was boycotted by some leading motorbike riders in the early 1970s. A number of important sponsors stayed away too. 30
The event is great for the island's economy, but not everybody likes it. I, for one, am not a motorbike fan. And I hate the crowds and the noise. But I have learned to live with it: I just book my holidays while the racing takes place. 35 That way, I can get away from the chaos of the races and enjoy the sun in Turkey or Spain. And the best thing is that I can pay for my holiday by renting out my little house to people who come to watch the TT race. 40

> • *First read the text.*
> • *Then do the tasks 1–5. Tick the correct box and* <u>*quote*</u> *from the text.*

1 In the TT event, the motorbikes race on a specially made race course.

This statement is … ☐ true. ☐ false. One piece of evidence from the text:

_____

2 During the TT race, roads on the Isle of Man can't be used for two weeks.

This statement is … ☐ true. ☐ false. One piece of evidence from the text:

_____

3 The number of motorbikes brought to the Isle of Man in 2015 was higher than 2014.

This statement is … ☐ true. ☐ false. One piece of evidence from the text:

_____

4 In the early 1970s there were no TT races.

This statement is …   ☐ true.   ☐ false.   One piece of evidence from the text:

_____

5 The writer who lives on the Isle of Man only sees disadvantages in the TT event.

This statement is …   ☐ true.   ☐ false.   One piece of evidence from the text:

_____

Indian food in Britain

Gemischte Aufgabenformate (Mixed tasks)

Indian cooking has been popular in Britain for a long time. Britain's first Indian restaurant opened its doors in 1810. In 1774 a British cookery book offered recipes for Indian dishes. Many
5   British people were familiar with Indian food because Britain controlled large parts of India. So British soldiers, administrators, engineers and their families spent many years of their lives in India. They started to like Indian food
10   and wanted more of it when they returned to Britain.

Back then it wasn't easy to buy fresh Indian spices in Britain. If they were imported from India, they spent up to six months in transport
15   by sea. They had often lost their flavour. So people experimented with spices from the Mediterranean or from Latin America. That's why the 'Indian' dishes in Britain tasted different than the originals in India.

20   What was easy to buy in Britain was a yellow powder called *curry powder*. It is a mix of dried spices. So the many individual flavourful dishes served in India became one standard dish called *curry* in Britain. In India you can't
25   buy *curry*. It would be as strange as asking for a soup in Europe without saying what sort of soup you want.

In the early 20th century, more and more people came to Britain from India. Many
30   immigrants were seamen who worked on British ships. They decided to stay in Britain when their ships returned to India.

Some of them opened small restaurants. They often came from countries now known as
35   Bangladesh and Pakistan. Back then, they were all part of British India, so their food was called Indian food. India became an independent country in 1948. Pakistan and Bangladesh later became independent countries too. Today, well
40   over half of all Indian restaurants in Britain have Bangladeshi owners and workers. But they are usually still called Indian.

The Indian restaurant owners soon realized that nobody in Britain was selling hot food late
45   at night. But people walking home after a drink in the pub or from a late shift at work wanted to buy hot food. These customers did not have time to sit down and eat. They wanted food that they could carry home. This was the birth of the
50   Indian take-away.

For years, *chicken tikka masala* was the most popular dish served in Indian takeaways. But a new trend is that customers are becoming more curious and trying out a wider range of
55   dishes. This is partly due to the influence of TV food programmes and comments on social media. Customers are now more informed about the variety of food available. Also, people are increasingly concerned about their health.
60   Many customers are looking for healthier dishes to eat.

> • *First read the text.*
> • *Then do the tasks 1–6.*
> • *For tasks 1, 3, 4 and 6 tick the correct box. Give evidence if the task asks for it. You <u>can</u> quote from the text.*
> • *For task 2 complete the sentence.*
> • *For task 5 decide if the statement is true or false and tick the correct box. Give evidence from the text.*

1 A British book from 1774 ...

    a) ☐ warned its readers against eating Indian food.

    b) ☐ told its readers how to prepare Indian food.

    c) ☐ explained how to open an Indian restaurant.

    One piece of evidence from the text: _____

    _____

2 Many British people liked Indian food in Britain 200 years ago because ...

    _____

3 Herbs and spices that were imported from India ...

    a) ☐ were often too expensive.

    b) ☐ often did not have much taste anymore.

    c) ☐ were too spicy for people in Britain.

4 You can't buy *curry* in India because ...

    a) ☐ you can't buy curry powder in India.

    b) ☐ you can only buy curry in Europe.

    c) ☐ there are a lot more dishes made with curry than in Britain.

5 Indian restaurants are often not really Indian.

    This statement is ... ☐ true. ☐ false.

    One piece of evidence from the text: _____

    _____

6 Indian restaurants started selling take-away food because ...

    a) ☐ people think it's healthier.

    b) ☐ they noticed that people wanted to buy freshly made meals on their way home.

    c) ☐ people did not sit down to eat any more.

Wortschatz – *Vocabulary*

1. Ablauf und Bewertung der Prüfung

Zweiter Prüfungsteil

Der Wortschatz ist – gemeinsam mit dem Leseverstehen und dem Schreiben – Teil des **zweiten Prüfungs-teils**. Für diese drei Fertigkeiten hast du insgesamt 70 Minuten Zeit. Hier kannst du deine zehn Minuten Bonuszeit nutzen, wenn du sie benötigst.

Ablauf beim Wortschatz

Im Abschnitt **Wortschatz** liest du einen Lückentext oder einzelne Sätze mit Lücken. Deine Aufgabe besteht darin, ein passendes Wort für jede Lücke zu finden. Manchmal gibt es eine *Multiple choice*-Auswahl oder einen Wortspeicher, manchmal musst du alle Wörter selbst finden. Bei *Matching*-Aufgaben musst du z. B. Wörtern eine passende Begriffserklärung zuordnen.

Bewertung beim Wortschatz

Der Bereich Wortschatz macht 15 % deiner Gesamtnote aus.

2. Typische Aufgabenformate in NRW

Im Folgenden lernst du typische Aufgabenformate kennen, die dich bei der Zentralen Prüfung 10 (ZP 10) im Bereich Wortschatz erwarten können. Die Tipp-Kästen enthalten nützliche Hinweise und Hilfen.

Making your own money

The following sentences are from a brochure about the job market in Britain.

Einsetzaufgaben (*Fill in the gap*)

Vom häufigsten Format im Wortschatzteil, den Einsetzaufgaben, gibt zwei verschiedene Varianten.

Einsetzaufgaben mit Auswahlmöglichkeit

> • *Complete the following text (sentences 1–5) with words from the box.*
> • *Use each word only once.*
> • *There is one more word than you need.*

understand	confidence	work	instead	employment	job

1   Research shows that most adults in Britain want to

_____ for their money.

2   Of course not everyone is able to find _____.

> **Tipp**
>
> Lies zunächst den ganzen Text. Du musst beim Ausfüllen nicht mit der ersten Lücke beginnen. Streiche jedes Wort, das du eingesetzt hast. So behältst du den Überblick.

> **Tipp**
>
> Erkläre dir unbekannte Begriffe mithilfe von Wörtern, die du kennst. *confidence*: Bestimmt kennst du *confident* (selbstbewusst), *confidence* bedeutet also _____. *employment*: Du weißt, was ein *employee* (Angestellter) ist? *Employment* könnte also _____ bedeuten!

> **Tipp**
>
> In Satz **2** könnten inhaltlich zwei Wörter passen: *job* und *employment*. Es heißt aber **nicht** *to find job*, sondern *to find* _____.

3 But most people _____ the advantages of having a job.

4 Having a job not only helps you to earn money but is also great for your _____.

5 And most people want to leave the house _____ of staying at home all day.

Einsetzaufgaben ohne Auswahlmöglichkeit

> - *Complete the following text (sentences 1–4) with suitable words.*
> - *Give only one solution.*

Tipp

Oft gibt es mehrere Wörter, die in eine Lücke passen könnten.

1 Many cafes and supermarkets offer *jobs* …
oder
1 Many cafes and supermarkets offer *work* …

Entscheide dich trotzdem für eine Lösung und trage sie ein.

1 Many cafes and supermarkets offer

_____ for people who are 16 or older.

2 That's great, because a lot of young people want to _____ their own money.

3 When they _____ enough money, they can spend it on things like travelling or a new smartphone.

4 Also, having some work _____ will look great on their future job applications!

Auswahlaufgaben (*Multiple choice*)

> - *Tick the correct box.*
> - *There is only one correct answer.*

Tipp

Bei vielen Aufgaben hilft dir auch dein Allgemeinwissen.
- Du weißt, dass es hier um *work* (Arbeit) und *working in teams* (Teamarbeit) geht.
- Du weißt, dass Teamarbeit gut für die Stimmung und die Qualität der Arbeit ist.
- a) *dangers* und c) *problems* haben eine negative Bedeutung.

Die richtige Lösung ist also _____.

1 When it comes to fun and productivity at work, we all know the

   a) ☐ dangers

   b) ☐ advantages

   c) ☐ problems

of working in teams.

2 However, team work is only great when all

   a) ☐ members

   b) ☐ partners

   c) ☐ parties

of the team do their part of the work.

Zuordnungsaufgaben *(Matching)*

> • *Match the words (1–4) with the definitions (A–D).*

1	work experience	**A**	the state of not having a job
2	employer	**B**	a person or company that pays people to work for them
3	apprenticeship	**C**	the work or jobs you have done in your life so far
4	unemployment	**D**	a period of time working and learning skills for a certain job

Tipp

Keine Panik, wenn du ein Wort nicht kennst!

Wenn du z. B. *unemployment* nicht kennst, erinnere dich daran, dass *un-* meistens etwas Negatives oder eine Verneinung bedeutet. In einer der Definitionen findest du das Wort *not*, ebenfalls eine Form der Verneinung. Die richtige Definition kann also nur _____ sein.

Ergänzungsaufgaben

> • *Fill the network with* <u>*eight job words*</u>*.*
> • *Write at least one word for each box.*

Tipp

Wenn acht Wörter verlangt werden, dann schreibe auf jeden Fall acht Wörter, auch wenn du unsicher bist. Bei der Punktevergabe gibt es Punkte sowohl für das richtige Wort als auch für die richtige Schreibweise!

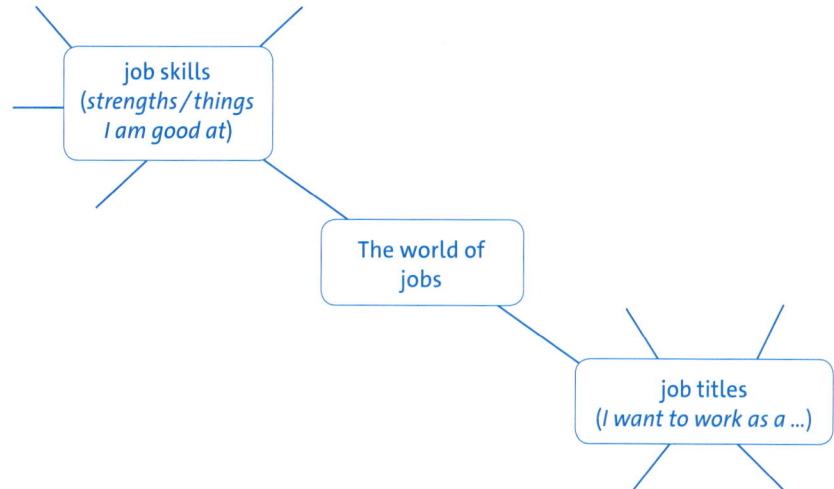

3. Wortschatz – *Now you*

Nun kannst du die Aufgabentypen und Strategien, die du auf den letzten Seiten kennen gelernt hast, gezielt üben.

My fear of going abroad

Auswahlaufgaben *(Multiple choice)*

> • *Tick the correct box.*
> • *There is only <u>one</u> correct answer.*

1 I was never any good at learning ...

   a) ☐ strange **b)** ☐ foreign **c)** ☐ fake **d)** ☐ irregular

   languages.

2 I started learning French in school, but my teacher had a terrible

   a) ☐ action **b)** ☐ accident **c)** ☐ accent **d)** ☐ accusation

   so I couldn't understand her.

3 My bad experience with learning languages at school made me

   a) ☐ nervous **b)** ☐ honest **c)** ☐ important **d)** ☐ spicy

   about travelling to another country.

4 If I get lost in another country, how can I ask somebody for

   a) ☐ diversity **b)** ☐ experience **c)** ☐ directions **d)** ☐ solutions

   if I do not speak the language?

5 But then, an

   a) ☐ exchange **b)** ☐ explained **c)** ☐ entertainment **d)** ☐ experience

   student from France came to my school.

6 We became friends and the following year, I spent my year

   a) ☐ outdoors **b)** ☐ backwards **c)** ☐ roundabout **d)** ☐ abroad

   in her family. It was great!

Gender equality

Einsetzaufgaben *(Fill in the gap)*

- *Complete the sentences 1–6 with suitable words from the box.*
- *Give only <u>one</u> solution.*
- *There ist <u>one more word</u> than you need.*

better	less	women	information	difference	agree	equal

1 These days we have more _____ about gender equality than ever before.

2 And most people _____ that gender equality is a good thing.

   But there are still some problems.

3 For example, girls often have _____ marks at school than boys.

4 And yet there are still too few _____ in top jobs.

5 And women are often paid _____ than men for the same job.

6 So, while in the past women demanded equal rights, they are now fighting for

   _____ pay.

Schreiben – *Writing*

1. Ablauf und Bewertung der Prüfung

Zweiter Prüfungsteil

Das **Schreiben** gehört – zusammen mit dem Leseverstehen und dem Wortschatz – zum **zweiten Prüfungsteil**, für den du insgesamt 70 Minuten zur Verfügung hast. Auch beim Schreiben kannst du deine zehn Minuten Bonuszeit nutzen, falls du mehr Zeit benötigst.

Ablauf beim Schreiben

In diesem Prüfungsteil schreibst du einen eigenen Text. Oft ist es ein beschreibender, berichtender oder erzählender Text (z. B. ein Erlebnisbericht, ein Tagebucheintrag oder eine E-Mail).
Manchmal wird dir ein kurzer Text (z. B. einen Brief, eine E-Mail oder eine Stellenanzeige) vorgegeben, auf den du mit deinem eigenen Text antworten musst. Die Aufgabenstellung kann aber auch lediglich konkrete Angaben für deinen Text enthalten.
Beide Möglichkeiten findest du in den folgenden Übungsaufgaben.

Bewertung beim Schreiben

Das Schreiben macht 45 % deiner Gesamtnote aus und ist somit ein sehr wichtiger Teil der Prüfung.
Die Punkte beim Schreiben werden für **Inhalt** und **Sprache** vergeben.

Der **Inhalt** im Prüfungsteil Schreiben zählt 17 % deiner Gesamtnote.

Die **Sprache** im Prüfungsteil Schreiben zählt 28 % deiner Gesamtnote.

Folgende Kriterien tragen zur Note für die Sprache bei:

- **Kommunikation:** Punkte dafür, dass du …
  - verständlich und lesbar schreibst,
  - deine Gedanken sinnvoll ordnest und dich nicht wiederholst,
  - die üblichen Regeln für die Textsorte (Brief, Blog, Bewerbung etc.) beachtest.

- **Ausdrucksvermögen:** Punkte dafür, dass du …
  - in deinen eigenen Worten schreibst und eine Vielfalt an Worten gebrauchst,
  - nicht ganze Sätze aus dem Text abschreibst, eigene Formulierungen verwendest,
  - komplexe Sätze bildest (mit Haupt- und Nebensätzen, *linking words*, *time phrases* etc.).

- **Sprachliche Korrektheit:** Punkte dafür, dass du …
  - die Wörter richtig schreibst,
  - die richtige Satzstellung und korrekte Zeitformen verwendest.

2. Typische Aufgabenformate in NRW

Im Folgenden lernst du typische Aufgabenformate kennen, die dich bei der Zentralen Prüfung 10 (ZP 10) im Bereich Schreiben erwarten können. Die Aufgaben verlangen Texte wie z. B. einen Brief, eine E-Mail oder einen kurzen Zeitungsartikel oder Blogeintrag. Es kann aber auch sein, dass du ein Bild beschreiben oder deine Meinung zu einem Thema vertreten sollst.
Die Tipp-Kästen enthalten nützliche Hinweise und Hilfen.

Write a letter or an email

Hier schreibst du einen Brief oder eine E-Mail, es handelt sich zum Beispiel um …
* einen persönlichen Brief
* einen Beschwerdebrief
* eine Bewerbung für einen Job.

> **Tipp**
>
> **Was ist bei Briefen und E-Mails zu beachten?**
> * Dein Schreiben muss zum Empfänger passen (Anrede, Schlussformel, Stil).
> * Merke dir ein paar der typischen Wendungen für **Briefe und E-Mails** (S. 31–36). Dann kannst du sie in der Prüfung verwenden.
> * **Bewerbungsschreiben** sind besonders.
>   → Deine Bewerbung muss zur Stellenanzeige passen.
>   → Du musst schreiben, für welchen Job du dich bewirbst und wo du die Anzeige gesehen hast.
>   → Schreibe auch, warum dich dieser Job interessiert und welche Qualifikationen du dafür mitbringst.
>   Natürlich darfst du beim Üben und in der Prüfung auch Angaben erfinden, sie sollten aber realistisch sein und müssen natürlich zum Job passen.

Schritt 1: Überlege, wer die Empfängerin oder der Empfänger ist. Wähle die richtige Anrede und Schlussformel. Fülle zur Wiederholung die Tabelle aus:

	Persönliches Schreiben	Offizielles (formelles) Schreiben
Anrede	*Hi (+name),*	Fall 1: Dear Mr / _____ / _____ (+ name) Fall 2: Dear Sir or _____
Schlussformel	*Bye for now,*	Fall 1: Yours _____ Fall 2: Yours _____

In **formellen** Briefen und E-Mails solltest du die Langform der Verben verwenden:

nicht: ~~I'd like to apply for the job.~~   sondern: *I would like to apply for the job.* _____

nicht: ~~I'll be away in August.~~   sondern: _____

nicht: ~~I'm in my last year at school.~~   sondern: _____

nicht: ~~I've worked in this cafe since June.~~   sondern: _____

nicht: ~~I don't mind working at weekends.~~   sondern: _____

Schritt 2: Wiederhole typische Formulierungen für die häufigsten Schreiben. Bearbeite dafür die folgenden Aufgaben.

a) Personal email

Die Prüfungsaufgabe kann zum Beispiel so aussehen:

Naima is your chat partner from Britain. Next year, she wants to come to your hometown for a few weeks to improve her German. You already exchanged a few emails.

Write an email to Naima giving information about your hometown.

In the email, ...

(1) ... write about:
- what makes your hometown special
- things young people can do in your town
- the disadvantages of your hometown for young people
- possible weekend trips and activities (what? where? when?)

(2) ... and ask one question about:
- when she will come to visit

or
- what she likes to do in her free time

Remember to include a nice beginning and a friendly ending.
Write about **120 words**.

1. Lies die Arbeitsanweisung genau durch und mache dir klar, welche Inhaltspunkte gefordert sind. Markiere Schlüsselwörter.
   Du verlierst Punkte, wenn du einen Inhaltspunkt übersiehst! Wenn du mehrere Arbeitsaufträge zur Auswahl hast, markiere die Aufträge, für die du dich entscheidest.

2. Prüfe genau, welche Textsorte von dir verlangt wird.
   Davon hängt die Anrede und die Grußformel ab.
   - **Persönliche Schreiben** sind z.B. Briefe und E-Mails an Freunde oder Verwandte.
   - **Offizielle/formelle Schreiben** sind z.B. Bewerbungsschreiben, Beschwerdebriefe oder Schreiben an Zeitungen, Radiosender, etc.

Tipp

Schau in dein Englischbuch oder in die Tabelle auf S. 31, falls du Hilfe bei diesen Redemitteln benötigst.

3. Überlege dir eine Struktur und mache dir Notizen, z.B. in einer Tabelle wie dieser.
   Die meisten Schreiben sind so gegliedert:

Einleitung	*I'm happy to hear that you want to come to ...*
Mittelteil	*My town is special, because ...* *Things to do:* *Bad things:* *Weekends:* *More information:*
Schluss	*When do you ... / Where do you want ... / What do you want ... / ...?*

► Fortsetzung (S. 33) nach den Lösungen

ABSCHLUSS-
PRÜFUNGS-
TRAINER
Nordrhein-Westfalen

Lösungen

Cornelsen

Hinweis zu den Lösungen:
Dieses Lösungsheft bietet Lösungen zu allen Aufgaben, verzichtet jedoch auf Lösungen zu den strategischen und oft individuellen Zwischenschritten in den Tipp-Kästen.

TRAINING SECTION: Hörverstehen ► S. 8 – 14

Calgary's skyways

Auswahlaufgaben (*Multiple choice*)
The underground cities in Canada ... **c)** *help people to stay warm in cold weather.*

Zuordnungsaufgabe (*Matching*)
1 Burlington: **C**
2 Stoney Creek: **B**
3 Kissimmee: **A**
4 Jacksonville: **E**
5 Jasper National Park: **D**

Einsetzaufgaben (*Fill in the gap*)
1 overhead
2 buildings

Kurzantwort-Aufgaben (*Giving short answers*)
1a) *They don't have to walk in the rain and cold. / are protected from the rain and cold. / are protected from the weather / ...*
b) *They don't have to cross the roads / are safe from the traffic. / are safer because they never have to cross a road. / ...*
2 Because there is less life in the streets. / less life at street level. / Because the streets feel deserted. / the streets are empty. / ...

The Niagara Falls

1c) *are for the most part in Canada.*
2 They wear clothes/coats/ponchos against the rain. / They wear waterproof ponchos/raincoats/...
3b) *was the first state park in the USA.*
4 she needed money / she was facing poverty.
5b) *injured.*
6a) *mainly* · *b)* *waterproof ponchos* · *c)* *the country's oldest* · *d)* *raise money* · *e)* *did hurt her head*

The Tour de Yorkshire

1c) *began in Yorkshire.*
2c) *there were old yellow bicycles on the sides of the road.*
3b) *didn't expect the positive reaction from people in Yorkshire.*
4b) *made people in Yorkshire want to see more cycling races.*
5a) *includes hills that are difficult even for experienced cyclists.*

Bob Marley

1 1: C · *2: A* · *3: D*
2 Bob Marley's first band was called "The Teenagers".
3 It was Number One in the Jamaican charts. / It was Nr 1 in Jamaica. / ...
4b) *he smoked cannabis and was politically active.*

TRAINING SECTION: Leseverstehen ► S. 15 – 24

Australia's Stolen Generation

Auswahlaufgaben mit Begründung
(*Multiple choice – with evidence from the text*)
Thousands of Aboriginal children ... **b)** *were stolen from their parents.*
One piece of evidence form the text: *"[...] to take Aboriginal children away from their mothers and fathers" (lines 3–4) / "[...] had to leave their homes" (lines 7–8)*

Einsetzaufgaben (*Fill in the gap*)
When Aboriginal children came to their new homes, they had to speak English.

Richtig / Falsch-Aufgaben mit Begründung (*True / False – with evidence from the text*)
true
One piece of evidence from the text: *..."[...] contact with their families, their language, their music and their way of life was broken off." (lines 4 ff.) / " [...] the children were not allowed contact with their families." (lines 2 ff.)*

Kasun

Zuordnungsaufgabe (*Matching*)
1 A · *2 D* · *3 C*

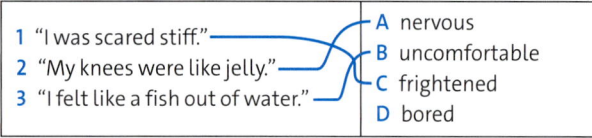

Kurzantwort-Aufgaben (*Giving short answers*)
1 (Because) he doesn't know if the big boy is talking/speaking to him.
2 He thinks that the big boy is going to / wants to / might hit him.
3 He stutters. / He talks too fast. / Sahan tells Kasun to calm down. / ...

Cartoon Strip

Sequenzierungsaufgaben (*Put in the right order*)
Picture 1: **C** · *Picture 2:* **A** · *Picture 3:* **B**

The Everglades

1 paragraph 1: **C** · *paragraph 2:* **D** · *paragraph 3:* **B**
2a) *watch alligator feedings. / watch alligators feeding. / see what alligators eat. / ...*
b) *learn about how the alligators' environment is endangered. / find out about the dangers that exist for the alligator's environment. / ...*
3a) *pollute the rivers and lakes with their dirty waste water. / let dirty water flow into the rivers and lakes. / ...*
b) *release their pets into the Everglades. / let their pets run into the Everglades. / allow their pets to go into the Everglades. / ...*
4a) *build a new bridge.*
b) *the water can pass under it (the bridge) and flow into the southern part of the Everglades.*

Filming in New Zealand

1a) *more than one region in New Zealand.*
2b) *in very different areas.*
3a) *is as big as the United Kingdom.*
4b) *looks a little bit like New York.*

The Isle of Man TT race

1 *false*
One piece of evidence from the text: "[...] it takes place on about 50 kilometres of our narrow public roads." (lines 8–9)
2 *true*
One piece of evidence from the text: "Every year the roads are closed to the public for a week of practice runs and a week of racing." (lines 10–11)
3 *true*
One piece of evidence from the text: "In 2015 about 36,0000 fans travelled to the Isle of Man. They brought over 14,000 motorbikes with them. That is 17 % more than the year before." (lines 17–20)
4 *false*
One piece of evidence from the text: "[...] the event was boycotted by some leading motorbike riders in the early 1970s." (lines 27–29)
5 *false*
One piece of evidence from the text: "But I have learned to live with it: I just book my holidays while the racing takes place. That way, I can get away from the chaos of the races and enjoy the sun in Turkey or Spain." (lines 34–37)

Indian food in Britain

1 b) *told its readers how to prepare Indian food.*
One piece of evidence from the text: "In 1774 a British cookery book contained recipes for Indian dishes." (lines 3–4)
2 *they had lived in India for a long time. / had spent many years of their lives in India. / ...*
3 b) *often did not have much taste anymore.*
4 c) *there are a lot more dishes made with curry than in Britain.*
5 *true*
One piece of evidence from the text: "Today, well over half of all Indian restaurants in Britain have Bangladeshi owners and workers." (lines 39–41)
6 b) *they noticed that people wanted to buy freshly made meals on their way home.*

TRAINING SECTION: Wortschatz ▶ S. 25–29

Making your own money

Einsetzaufgaben (*Fill in the gap*)
1 *work*
2 *employment*
3 *understand*
4 *confidence*
5 *instead*

Einsetzaufgaben ohne Auswahlmöglichkeiten
1 *jobs/work*
2 *earn/make*
3 *save/have/earn*
4 *experience*

Auswahlaufgaben (*Multiple choice*)
1 b) *advantages*
2 a) *members*

Zuordnungsaufgaben (*Matching*)
1: C · 2: B · 3: D · 4: A

Ergänzungsaufgaben
job skills (strengths / things I am good at): confident/confidence, friendly/friendliness, reliable, honest, punctual, dynamic, independent, organising, structuring, serving customers, proof-reading, communication, motivating others, team-work ...
job titles: mechanic, hair dresser, nurse, doctor, teacher, shop assistant, painter, animal care assistant, lawyer, musician, actor/actress, waiter/waitress, writer, director, cook, paramedic, florist, software engineer, ...

My fear of going abroad

1 b) *foreign*
2 c) *accent*
3 a) *nervous*
4 c) *directions*
5 a) *exchange*
6 d) *abroad*

Gender equality

1 *information*
2 *agree*
3 *better*
4 *women*
5 *less*
6 *equal*

TRAINING SECTION: Schreiben ▶ S. 30–39

Write a letter or an email

	Persönliches Schreiben	Offizielles (formelles) Schreiben
Anrede	*Hi (+name),* *Dear (+ name)*	*Fall 1: Dear Mr/Mrs/Ms (+ name)* *Fall 2: Dear Sir or Madam*
Schluss-formel	*By for now, See you soon, Love, ...*	*Fall 1: Yours sincerely* *Fall 2: Yours faithfully*

I would like to apply for the job.
I will be away in August.
I am in my last year at school.
I have worked in this café since June.
I do not mind working at weekends.

a) Personal email
4. ~~here~~: *hear* · ~~while~~: *because* · ~~have~~: *has* · ~~has it~~: *it has* · ~~swiming~~: *swimming* · ~~don't~~: *doesn't* · ~~who~~: *where* · ~~interested~~: *interesting* · ~~will~~: *want to*

b) Letter of complaint (about an online order)
Dear Sir or Madam,
I ordered a phone on Friday 3rd May. But when it arrived here the front was broken. / the charger was missing. / it didn't work.
I am very unhappy with this service. Please can you send me the missing charger. / a new phone.
I will then return the phone / the charger that you sent me.
Many thanks for your cooperation.
Yours faithfully
Callum Spencer

c) Letter of complaint (to a hotel)

1. Dear Mrs Turner

2. I stayed in your hotel from 1st to 5th May.

3. But I was very unhappy with my room.

4. To begin with, the bathroom/shower/floor was dirty. Then there weren't any towels/clean sheets/pillows. What's more, it was very noisy because people were repairing the front of the hotel.
And finally, the brochure promised a view of the sea, but I couldn't see the sea.

5. So what can you offer me to make up for my bad experience? I would like to ask to get part of my money back for my stay at your hotel.

6. I look forward to hearing from you soon.

7. Yours sincerely,
Zoe Smith

d) Letter of application (for a job)

Dear Sir or Madam
I read your advert online/in a magazine/in a newspaper and would like to apply for the job of assistant to help in your café this summer.
I am in year 10 at the Rheingau School in Dortmund.
I had 8 years of English lessons in school. A summer job in your café would give me the chance to improve my English.
I already have some experience because last year I worked in a café in my hometown of Dortmund.
My responsibilities included taking orders and making coffee and sandwiches.
I am honest and reliable. I like working with people.
I speak German as my first language, and I also speak English.
I could start work in July/on Monday.
Please find my CV attached.
I look forward to hearing from you soon.
Yours faithfully
…

Articles

Beispiellösung:

My Swedish adventure

Last year, we went to Sweden on our summer holiday. I enjoyed it very much.
We went up the east coast by car and visited many small villages on our way up to Stockholm. When we arrived in the capital, it was raining but there were still a lot of things to do. We went to an amazing museum where we learned about an old ship called the Vasa. It sunk in the Stockholm harbor a long time ago. But it was taken out of the water so that people could look at it.
On our way back to Germany it was very windy. So we stopped at a big beach and flew our kite. That was probably the best experience, we had so much fun!
I really want to go there again next summer.

(138 Wörter)

Blogs

Beispiellösung:

We use social media every day. At least, the younger generation does. I, for example, use it mostly for communicating with friends and family.
Some people say that the younger generation doesn't talk to people face to face anymore and that they hide behind the screen instead of talking in the real world. For some people this might be true. But I don't really think this way. I still see my friends every day in real life. But we prefer to discuss the time and place we want to meet at by texting each other instead of talking on the phone.
So I see social media more as an addition to face to face communication. It also helps me to keep in touch with friends who don't live in the same city or country when face to face communication is simply not possible.

(144 Wörter)

Describing a picture

Beispiellösung:

The picture shows a group of young people on a holiday.
In the middle of the picture you can see a campfire. There are hills and a lake in the background.
In the picture, there are five people are sitting around a fire. The girl to the left is wrapped in a blanket and another girl is wearing a hat. Everyone is wearing warm clothes.
All the people in the picture are laughing. They are holding cups and two of them are roasting marshmallows over the fire.
I think the people are on a holiday in the mountains. Maybe they are there to go hiking and camping. It could be cold there because they are sitting around a fire.
I would also like to go on an adventure holiday because I really like hiking. But I don't like camping. I like sleeping in a real bed especially when it's not summer. Maybe sleeping in a hut would be more comfortable.

(158 Wörter)

Schreiben – *Now you*

a) Beispiellösung:

Dear Sir or Madam
A couple of days ago I bought one of your cameras online. It arrived this morning and I wanted to try it. Unfortunately, the camera is not working. I charged it, but when I pressed the start button nothing happened. I tried it more than once. The packaging of the camera was damaged, too. It looks like the camera has been used before already. This is unacceptable. I am very unhappy with this service. Could you please send me a new and working camera? I will send the other one back and hope you will pay for the shipping costs as well.
Thank you very much for your help in advance.
Yours faithfully
…

(118 Wörter)

b) Beispiellösung:

Dear Sir or Madam

I read your advert online and would like to apply for the job as a dog walker.

I am 16 years old and I would like to earn some money after school in the afternoon.

I love animals and have already some experience with dog walking because I have a dog myself. I take my dog out every day after school so it would be easy for me to take other dogs with me as well.

I can pick the dogs up on my way to the park and bring them back whenever is best for the owner.

I am a reliable and friendly person.

I could start work as soon as possible and am free every afternoon except for the weekends.

Please find my CV attached.

I look forward to hearing from you.

Yours faithfully

…

(140 Wörter)

c) Beispiellösung:

Last summer, I went to Edinburgh for a language camp. It was not difficult to organize because the camp organization helped me a lot with the planning.

In Edinburgh, I was staying with a host family. That was really good because I had to speak English with my host family all the time.

But I wasn't at home much because we had English lessons in the morning and then we went on trips and had fun events in the afternoon with all the other members of the camp. The lessons were better than school lessons because we always played fun games and the teachers were native speakers. We learned many new words and some facts about the city. It was a great experience and I improved my English skills a lot.

I would recommend the language camp!

(137 Wörter)

MUSTERPRÜFUNG 1: Hörverstehen ▶ S. 42–43

Bo Kaap – a special district in Cape Town

1 a) more than hundred years ago.
2 Britain / (the) Netherlands
3 b) are Asian.
4 a) They worked in sugar fields.
b) They worked in coal mines.
5 c) gives information about the Asian population of Cape Town.
6 ... painted in very bright colours. / very colourful.

A presentation about William Shakespeare

1 b) but you can still see his plays in many theatres today.
2 c) had two daughters and a son.
3 His son died. / ...when he was a child. / ...when he was eleven.
4 1: B · 2: D · 3: A
5 They were made of wood. / had very low ceilings. / had very small windows.
6 b) is a modern copy of the theatre from Shakespeare's days.

MUSTERPRÜFUNG 1: Leseverstehen ▶ S. 44–45

High-rise living in Britain

1 c) often in poor condition.
2 true:
One piece of evidence from the text: "...they feel safer than in a house. After all, nobody can climb through the window of a flat on the 16th floor." (lines 15–17)
3 b) there are fewer insects or other small animals than in houses.
One piece of evidence from the text: "And there are almost no mice, ants and spiders in the flats." (lines 18–19)
4 false
One piece of evidence from the text: "It is true that families with children still like to live in a house with a front door ..." (lines 30–31)
5 b) helps people become older.
6 true
One piece of evidence from the text: "If we want to protect our environment ..." (line 57)

MUSTERPRÜFUNG 1: Wortschatz ▶ S. 46–47

The joys of travelling

Teil 1
1 deal
2 station
3 alternative
4 frustrating
5 annoyed
6 solve

Teil 2
1 situations/moments/problems
2 forget
3 learn
4 different/new/interesting
5 compass/map
6 enjoy/like/love

MUSTERPRÜFUNG 1: Schreiben ▶ S. 48

Beispiellösung:
Hi Ben
Thanks for your email. I am glad that you are well and that you like your job.
I am good as well. I want to save some money for travelling so I also have a job: I am a private tutor. I help younger students with their homework in English, German and Biology.
Sometimes it can be hard if you have to explain something more than once, for example. You really need to try and find different ways to explain the same thing so that everyone understands it. But I love talking to other people so I think I have the right job.
I really enjoy it. I would hate to sit in an office all day and work all by myself.
Looking forward to hearing from you soon!
Take care,
...

(133 Wörter)

MUSTERPRÜFUNG 2: Hörverstehen ▶ S. 49–50

Two sights in Brighton

1 c) it is not often warm enough to go swimming.
2 162 metres / The British Airways i360 / It is 162 metres high.
3 expensive
4 The water came from the streets. / ... the kitchens. / ... the bathrooms. / ... the toilets.
5 c) they prevent people from getting sick.
6 12 / over 11 / older than 11 (years old) / You have to be 12. / ... over 11. / ... older than 11 (years old).

Cricket in India

1 c) have the most fans
2 a) was low in 1975 and is now higher.
3 c) is less succesful in cricket than Australia.
4 a) are Indian and play in Indian teams.
5 a) think that cricket is not a real sport.
6 The games are shorter now. / It has a different name now. / It is more exciting now.

MUSTERPRÜFUNG 2: Leseverstehen ▶ S. 51–52

Stereotypically Irish?

1 false
One piece of evidence from the text: "It turns out that these stereotypes are not helpful at all if you want to know who the Irish are today." (lines 7–9)
2 c) in the U.S. than in Ireland.
3 false
One piece of evidence from the text: "Chefs in Irish restaurants are modernising traditional dishes by mixing fresh local products with exciting ingredients and flavours from all over the world." (lines 25–29)
4 c) are family places, too.
5 c) is going down.
6 b) are getting divorced less frequently

How shopping has changed

Teil 1
1 *husband*
2 *meat/food/things*
3 *helped/served/assisted*
4 *customers*
5 *groceries*
6 *take*

Teil 2
1 *environment*
2 *instead*
3 *floors*
4 *growth*
5 *search*
6 *result*

Come work at Trifdon Castle

Beispiellösung:
Dear Sir or Madam
I read your advert online and would like to apply for the job as a shop assistant.
I am 16 years old and will finish school this summer. I have already worked as a shop assistant in a small town in Germany last summer. I mainly worked at the till.
I speak German as my first language and I also speak English. I would very much like to work in the souvenir shop in Trifdon Castle because I would like to improve my English and because I am very interested in history.
I am a communicative person. My general interests are reading, swimming and playing the guitar.
Attached you will find my CV.
I look forward to hearing from you soon.
Yours faithfully
…

(127 Wörter)

The Pennymoore Day Centre is looking for assistant helpers!

Beispiellösung:
Dear Sir or Madam
I read your advert online and would like to apply for the job as an assistant helper at Pennymoore Day Centre.
I am 16 years old and I will finish school this summer. I am a reliable person and I like to communicate. I enjoy cooking and baking in my free time.
I would very much like to support your team because I like helping other people. I would also like to improve my English skills. My first language is German, but I learned English in school.
I have worked in a café before. My responsibilities included serving the customers and doing the grocery shopping.
Attached you will find my CV.
I look forward to hearing from you soon.
Yours faithfully
…

(120 Wörter)

The D of E expedition

1 *Because the ground was very hard. / wasn't exactly / very soft.*
2 *b) is missing one of her shoes.*
3 *adventure*
4 *On the silver level …*
A *you're on an expedition for three days and two nights.*
C *you need more to eat and to wear than on the bronze level.*
5 *a) to call for help.*
6 *They walked around the same field twice.*

A presentation about Wales

1 *b) played better than England.*
2 *They say "I'm Welsh". / They say they are Welsh.*
3 *c) not like English at all.*
4 *road signs*
5 *a) lots of farm animals.*
6 *b) built by an English king.*

Good health in Australia?

1 *false*
One piece of evidence from the text: "… the lifeguards […] are all young, healthy and athletic" (lines 9–10)
2 *b) give a positive picture of Australia.*
3 *Because of the sun …*
A *people needed to start wearing sun protection.*
C *a high number of Australians got skin cancer.*
4 *false*
One piece of evidence from the text: "On average, Australians are now as heavy as as people in the USA." (lines 42–43)
5 *a) do not get enough exercise*
6 *true*
One piece of evidence from the text: "… the problems of skin cancer and extra kilos contrast with Australia's image of fitness and health." (lines 57–59)

Life in the outback

Teil 1
1 *b) population*
2 *b) similar*
3 *d) building*
4 *a) even*
5 *c) blocked*
6 *a) consequence*

Teil 2
1 *hand*
2 *water/rain*
3 *problems*
4 *children*
5 *lonely/alone*
6 *important/essential*

MUSTERPRÜFUNG 3: Schreiben   ▶ S. 62

Beispiellösung:

Dear Sir or Madam
a couple of weeks ago, I ordered a tablet from your website.
It arrived today.
Unfortunately, I am very unhappy with your service.
Firstly, the tablet arrived three weeks later than expected.
Moreover, the box around the tablet was broken and half open so
that the tablet was not protected properly. There was also a
scratch on the display. Last but not least, the charger was missing.
This is unacceptable. Could you please send me a new tablet with
a charger as soon as possible? I will then send the broken tablet
to your company. I hope that the tablet arrives sooner this time.
Thank you very much in advance for your help.
Yours faithfully

...

(120 Wörter)

Notentabelle

Punkte	Note
87–100	sehr gut
73–86	gut
59–72	befriedigend
45–58	ausreichend
18–44	mangelhaft
0–17	ungenügend

4. Wie könnte deine Lösung aussehen? Hier ist ein Beispiel. Aber Achtung: Die blau markierten Wörter sind falsch.
Lies die Hinweise und verbessere die Fehler.

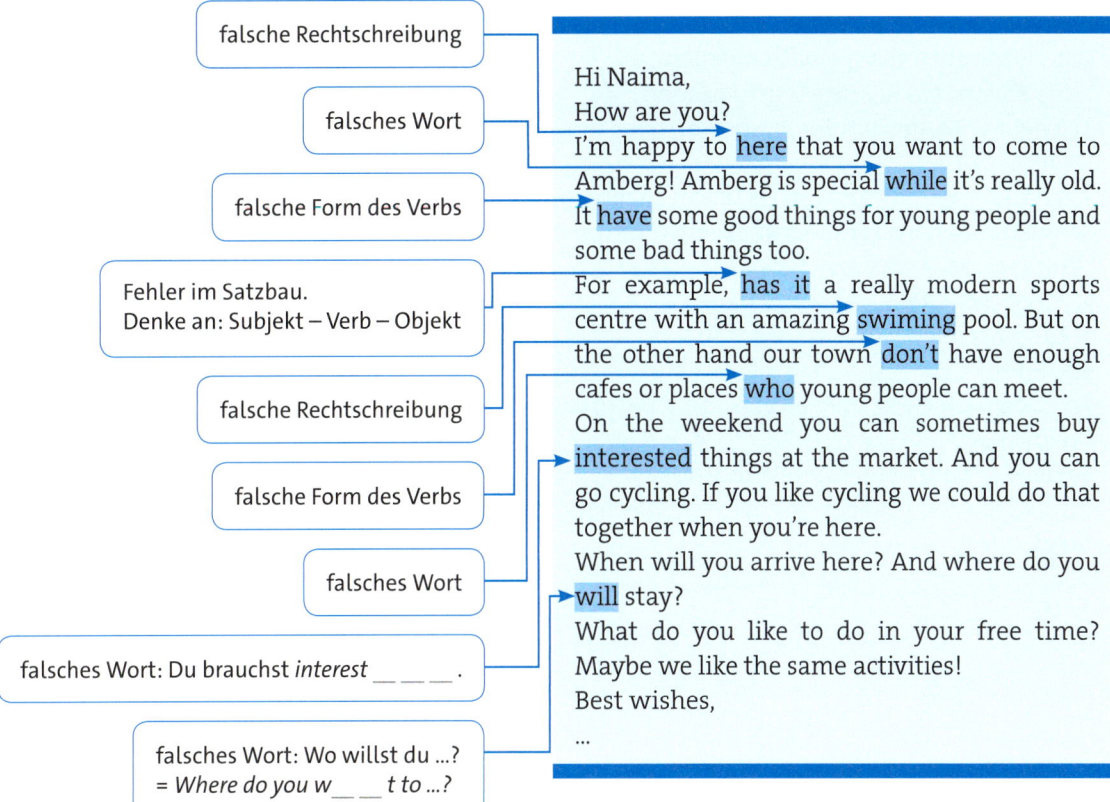

falsche Rechtschreibung

falsches Wort

falsche Form des Verbs

Fehler im Satzbau.
Denke an: Subjekt – Verb – Objekt

falsche Rechtschreibung

falsche Form des Verbs

falsches Wort

falsches Wort: Du brauchst *interest* _ _ _ _ .

falsches Wort: Wo willst du …?
= *Where do you w_ _ _ t to …?*

> Hi Naima,
> How are you?
> I'm happy to here that you want to come to Amberg! Amberg is special while it's really old. It have some good things for young people and some bad things too.
> For example, has it a really modern sports centre with an amazing swiming pool. But on the other hand our town don't have enough cafes or places who young people can meet.
> On the weekend you can sometimes buy interested things at the market. And you can go cycling. If you like cycling we could do that together when you're here.
> When will you arrive here? And where do you will stay?
> What do you like to do in your free time? Maybe we like the same activities!
> Best wishes,
> …

b) Letter of complaint (about an online order)

Fülle die Lücken in diesem Beschwerdebrief mit Begriffen aus dem Kasten.

arrived • missing • ordered • broken • return • send • work • sent • unhappy • Sir or Madam • on • cooperation • thanks • faithfully

Dear

I _____ a phone _____ Friday 3rd May.

But when it _____ here the front was

_____ ./the charger was _____ ./

it didn't _____ .

I am very _____ with this service.

Please can you _____ me the missing charger./

_____ a new phone.

I will then _____ the phone/the charger that

you _____ me.

Many _____ for your _____ .

Yours _____

Callum Spencer

c) Letter of complaint (to a hotel)

Schau dir die Struktur eines typischen Beschwerdebriefes an (Seite 33).
Bringe die Sätze aus dem Beispielbrief in die richtige Reihenfolge (1–7) und schreibe sie auf die vorgegebenen Zeilen.

But I was very unhappy with my room.
I look forward to hearing from you soon.
To begin with, the bathroom / shower / floor was dirty.
Dear Ms Turner
Then there weren't any towels / clean sheets / pillows.
So what can you offer me to make up for my bad experience?
What's more, it was very noisy because people were repairing the front of the hotel.
Yours sincerely
~~Zoe Smith~~
And finally, the brochure promised a view of the sea, but I couldn't see the sea.
I stayed in your hotel from 1st to 5th May.
I would like to ask to get part of my money back for my stay at your hotel.

> **Tipp**
>
> **Anrede von Frauen in formellen Briefen:**
> - *Ms* ist eine neutrale Anrede für alle Frauen und passt immer!
> - *Mrs* galt früher als Anrede für verheiratete Frauen. Heute ist diese Anrede in formellen Briefen nicht mehr so üblich.

1. Anrede: *Dear* _____

2. Schreibe, wann du im Hotel warst:

   _____

3. Schreibe, dass du unzufrieden bist:

   _____

4. Gib die Gründe für deine Unzufriedenheit an:

   _____

   _____

   _____

5. Frage, was dir das Hotel anbieten kann oder mache einen Vorschlag:

   _____

6. Schreibe einen Schlusssatz:

   _____

7. Abschiedsformel: _____

   Zoe Smith

d) Letter of application (for a job)

Die Prüfungsaufgabe für ein Bewerbungsschreiben kann z. B. so aussehen:

You are planning to get a summer job in Britain after leaving school. You found the following two job adverts online.
- Read the job adverts.
- Choose one job you want to apply for.

Do you love animals?

Come work at Grantham Animal Shelter!

We are looking for young people to help us feed our animals, play and cuddle with them and clean their cages.

If you are
- 16 or older,
- kind to animals,
- responsible and reliable,
- and willing to work hard and get your hands dirty ...
... apply now!

Send your application to:
granthamshelter@example.com

The Corner Café is looking for servers!

Would you like to join our team?

Then you should ...
- be 16 or older,
- like working in a team,
- be friendly and open towards other people,
- have some work experience in a restaurant or café.

We can offer you ...
- a relaxed and joyful working atmosphere,
- a good pay, plus additional tips.

If you are interested, contact:
thecorner@example.com

Write an email application.
Include the following information:
- personal details
- general interests
- your motivation for the job you chose
- your qualifications

Write about **120 words**.
Remember the formal characteristics of a letter of application.

Tipp

Bewerbungsschreiben sind meist so aufgebaut:

Dear Sir or Madam / Dear Mr/Ms (+ name)

I read/saw your advert (+ where and/or when) and I would like to apply for the job (+ which job?).

(Introduce yourself.)

(Say something about your experience and/or qualifications and your qualities as a person.)

(Say why you really want the job.)

(Say when you could start.)

(Give information about your references and CV.)

I look forward to hearing from you soon.

Yours faithfully/sincerely

(+ your name)

Fülle die **blauen** Lücken mit Wörtern aus dem Kasten. Ergänze in den **grauen** Lücken deine eigenen Angaben.

apply • advert • forward • faithfully • improve • experience • language • CV

Tipp

Auch hier müssen die Informationen über dich, deine Interessen und deine Berufserfahrung nicht wahr sein. Lass deiner Fantasie freien Lauf! Achte aber darauf, dass die Angaben zum Job passen.

Dear Sir or Madam

I read your _____ online / in a magazine / in a newspaper and I would like

to _____ for the job of assistant to help in your cafe this summer.

I am in year 10 at the _____ in _____ .

I had _____ years of English lessons in school. A summer job in your cafe would give me

the chance to _____ my English.

I already have some _____ because last year I _____

_____ .

My responsibilities included taking orders and making coffee and sandwiches.

I am honest and _____ . I like working with _____ .

I speak _____ as my first _____ , and I also speak

_____ .

I could start work in/on _____ .

Please find my _____ attached.

I look _____ to hearing from you soon.

Yours _____

_____

Articles

Manche Aufgaben verlangen das Schreiben eines Artikels, z. B. für eine Schulzeitung oder eine Website. Das Thema für den Artikel wird dir vorgegeben, häufig geht es z. B. um vergangene, aktuelle oder zukünftige Themen rund um Schule und Freizeit. Manchmal wird auch eine Meinungsäußerung von dir verlangt. Ein Artikel ist meist in einer sachlichen Sprache verfasst. Denke aber auch daran, wo dein Artikel erscheint und wer ihn lesen wird. Wenn du für Gleichaltrige schreibst, kann dein Ton natürlich lockerer sein, als wenn du ein breiteres Publikum oder Erwachsene ansprichst.

Die Prüfungsaufgabe kann zum Beispiel so aussehen:

The newspaper team at your Irish partner school asked students to write about their favourite summer holiday.

Write an article for the school newspaper about your best summer vacation.

In your **article** include **at least three** of the following aspects:

- where you went on vacation
- what you learned from the trip
- special experiences (good/interesting/bad) on the trip
- whether you would go there again or not.

Write about 120 words.

Tipp

Keine Panik, wenn du zu einem Thema keine eigene Erfahrung hast. Hier ist bloß Fantasie gefragt – du darfst alles frei erfinden.

Bevor du beginnst: Lies die Aufgabenstellung genau. Mache dir klar, was genau von dir verlangt wird.

Schritt 1: Mache dir Notizen. Beachte dabei die von dir verlangten Inhalte (drei oder mehr Aspekte).

where I went	special experiences	what I learned	Will I go there again?

Schritt 2: Schreibe nun deinen Text. Verwende dabei deine Notizen. Die Reihenfolge, in der du die vier Aspekte abarbeitest, spielt keine Rolle. Um deinen Text auch optisch zu strukturieren, beginne für jeden Aspekt einen neuen Absatz.

Blogs

Blogs sind persönliche Texte. Deshalb hast du beim Verfassen eines Blogs gewisse sprachliche Freiheiten. Meistens enthält die Aufgabe genaue Angaben zu Aspekten, die du in deinem Blog-Eintrag erwähnen sollst. Auch hier wird manchmal eine Meinungsäußerung von dir verlangt.

Die Prüfungsaufgabe kann zum Beispiel so aussehen:

You have found the following post on the Internet:

Are social media keeping us from talking face to face?
Young people can't live without social media and use them to communicate with their friends all the time. But are social media keeping them from talking face to face to the people around them?

Write an <u>entry on this blog</u> giving your opinion. Write about:
- your personal experience with social media,
- your experience of how you communicate with or without using social media,
- whether or not you think that social media are keeping you from face to face communication.

Write about 120 words.

personal experience with social media	my communication habits (with / without) social media	Are social media keeping us from real life communication?

Schritt 2: Schreibe nun deinen Text. Verwende dabei deine Notizen.

Tipp

In einem Blog hast du mehr sprachliche Freiheiten, z. B. sind in einem Blog manchmal auch unvollständige Sätze erlaubt. Beispiel:

I would never leave the house without my smartphone.

→ Going out without my smartphone? Never!

Tipp

Folgende Formulierungen können dir helfen, deine eigene Meinung zu einem Thema auszudrücken:

In my opinion/experience …
I definitely/really (don't) think that …
On the one hand, I (don't) think that …
On the other hand, …
However, it's also true that …
I'm in favour of … because …
Many people say that … / are in favour of …
I agree/disagree with the opinion that …

Schritt 3: Überprüfe jetzt deinen Text. Dafür kannst du die folgende Checkliste verwenden:

Checkliste:	
Hat der Text die geforderte Länge (ungefähr 120 Wörter)?	☐
Gibt es einen passenden Anfang und Schluss?	☐
Sind alle Aspekte aus der Aufgabenstellung enthalten?	☐
Verbindungswörter: Hast du die Sätze in deinem Text mit sinnvollen Verbindungswörtern verbunden?	☐
Satzstellung: Prüfe die Satzstellung und bei jedem Verb die Zeitform (Gegenwart oder Vergangenheit).	☐
Rechtschreibung: Prüfe, ob du alle Wörter richtig geschrieben hast. Wenn du unsicher bist, versuche den Satz umzuformulieren.	☐
Stil: Passt der Stil des Schreibens zum Leser und zur Textsorte?	☐

Describing a picture

Die Prüfungsaufgabe kann z. B. so aussehen:

You are planning a summer vacation with your British friends. On the internet page of a travel agency you found these two pictures. Now you tell your friends about the pictures and where you want to go.

Choose one of the pictures and **describe** it. In your description, you should include the following aspects:

- the general situation in the picture
- details about what you see in the picture
- what the people in the picture are doing and where you think they are
- whether you would/wouldn't like to go there

Write about 120 words.

Beim Beschreiben von Bildern kannst du so vorgehen:

1. Schreibe etwas über das allgemeine Thema des Bildes (*topic sentence*):
   The picture shows a group of young people on a holiday.
   In the picture, a group of young are people on a holiday.

2. Beschreibe das Bild genauer:
   I can see a campfire in the middle of the picture.
   There are hills and a lake in the background.

3. Beschreibe, was die Personen gerade tun. Verwende dafür das *present progressive* (Verb + *ing*):
   *In the picture, five people **are sitting** around a fire.*
   *They **are wearing** ...*
   *The people in the picture **are laughing**.*

4. Überlege, wo die Personen sich aufhalten könnten.
   ***I think** the people are on a holiday in the mountains.*
   ***Maybe** they are there to go hiking and camping.*
   It could be cold there, because ...

5. Sage deine Meinung zum Thema des Bildes:
   I would like to go on an adventure holiday, because I really like hiking. But I don't like camping. I like sleeping in a real bed.

Tipp

Was tun, wenn dir ein englisches Wort nicht einfällt? Gib nicht gleich auf!
- Du kannst das Wort vielleicht um-schreiben (Foto B):
  The woman in the picture is swimming underwater. (→ *diving/snorkeling*)
  She is wearing special glasses. (→ *diving goggles*)
- Wenn dir das Gegenteil einfällt, kannst du es verneinen (Foto A):
  The area does not look noisy at all.
  (→ *quiet, peaceful*)
Verwende jedoch keine deutschen Wörter, wenn dir das englische nicht einfällt.

Tipp

Wiederhole die Ortsangaben zur Bild-beschreibung:
In the foreground/background I can see ...
On the left/right there is/are ...
At the bottom/top/centre ...
In the top left/right corner ...
In the left/right bottom corner ...
There is/are ... next to ... / behind ... /
in front of ... / opposite ... / between ...

3. Schreiben – *Now you*

Schreibe eine E-Mail, einen Brief und einen Artikel für die Schülerzeitung. Schreibe je ca. 120 Wörter.

a) You bought a camera from an American online shop, but there is something wrong with it. Write an email to complain about it.

b) You have read an advert for a job as a dog walker. Write a letter to apply for the job.

c) Last summer, you went to a language camp in Britain. Now the camp organization has asked you to write an article about your experience for their newsletter.

Schritt 4: Überprüfe und verbessere deine Texte.

- Vergleiche deine E-Mail mit Beispiel **b)** (S. 33).
- Vergleiche deinen Brief mit Beispiel **d)** (S. 35–36).
- Prüfe deinen Zeitungsartikel mit der Checkliste (S. 30).

Tipp

Es ist immer leichter, Fehler bei anderen zu finden! Eine sehr gute Übung ist also, fremde Texte zu überprüfen. So trainierst du die Fähigkeit, auch in deinen eigenen Texten Fehler zu sehen.

Tipps für die Prüfung

Prüfungsvorbereitung

- **Beginne rechtzeitig mit dem Lernen. Mache dir einige Wochen vor der Prüfung einen Plan.** Plane Wiederholungsphasen ein. Starte mit Aufgaben, die dir im Unterricht noch schwerfallen. Hake ab, was du bereits erledigt hast.

- **Überlege dir, wo du im Englischen noch grundsätzliche Probleme oder Lücken hast** (z. B. Grammatikprobleme, die immer wieder auftreten). Diese Themen kannst du dann mit den interaktiven Übungen auf www.scook.de gezielt noch einmal wiederholen.

- **Mache dich mit dem Ablauf der Prüfung und mit allen Aufgabenformaten vertraut.** Plane im Vorfeld, wie viel Zeit du für jeden Prüfungsteil und für die Kontrolle zur Verfügung hast.

- **Schreibe dir auf, wann und wo die Prüfung stattfindet**, und plane etwas mehr Zeit für den Weg ein als sonst.

- **Lege alle Materialien am Vorabend der Prüfung bereit** (z. B. funktionstüchtige Stifte, Uhr – Smartphones und Wörterbücher sind <u>nicht</u> erlaubt!).

- **Achte auf ausreichend Schlaf und ein gutes Frühstück.**

Wenn du dich gut vorbereitet hast, kannst du selbstbewusst in die Prüfung gehen!

Während der Prüfung

- **Behalte die Zeit im Blick!** Am besten legst du während der Prüfung eine Uhr auf den Tisch und schaust von Zeit zu Zeit darauf. Wenn dir eine Aufgabe schwerfällt, gehe lieber erstmal zur nächsten Frage weiter. Nimm dir am Ende einige Minuten Zeit, um deine Antworten noch einmal durchzugehen.

- **Lies die Aufgabenstellung gründlich durch**, bevor du mit der Bearbeitung beginnst. Manchmal enthält eine Aufgabe mehrere Teilaspekte. **Markiere** sie und übersetze sie dir zur Sicherheit in deine Muttersprache.

- **Nutze deine Chance!** Auch wenn du unsicher bist, ob die Lösung stimmt, solltest du die Aufgabe trotzdem bearbeiten. Kreuzt du keine Lösung an oder lässt die Lücke leer, bekommst du auf jeden Fall null Punkte.

- **Mache dir bei Schreibaufgaben Notizen, wenn du genug Zeit hast.** Sie können dir helfen, deine Gedanken zu ordnen und deinen Text sinnvoll zu strukturieren. Beachte aber, dass **nur dein endgültiger Text in die Bewertung eingeht**.

- **Gib deinen Texten eine gute Struktur mit Einleitung, Hauptteil und Schluss.** Beginne jeden neuen Textteil mit einem neuen Absatz.

- **Formuliere klare Sätze.** Vermeide es, deutsche Sätze wortwörtlich ins Englische zu übersetzen. Formuliere möglichst mit deinen eigenen Worten, es sei denn, die Aufgabenstellung verlangt ein Zitat aus dem Text (z. B. „One piece of evidence from the text:", „Give examples from the text.").

- **Kontrolliere am Ende**, was du geschrieben hast. Achte besonders auf Vollständigkeit, die Rechtschreibung, die Zeitformen deiner Verben und den Satzbau.

Wir wünschen dir viel Erfolg für deine Prüfung!

ABSCHLUSS-PRÜFUNGS-TRAINER

Nordrhein-Westfalen

Musterprüfungen

Erster Prüfungsteil: Hörverstehen

1. Hörverstehen – Teil 1

Bo-Kaap – a special district in Cape Town

A tourist guide is giving a tour of the Bo-Kaap district in Cape Town, South Africa.

> - *First read the tasks 1–6.*
> - *Then listen to the guide.*
> - *While you are listening, tick the correct box, answer the question or fill in the information.*
> - *At the end you will hear the guide again.*
> - *Now read the tasks 1–6. You have **one minute** to do this.*

A street in Bo-Kaap with a mosque

> - *Now listen to the guide and do the tasks.*

1 The Bo-Kaap mosque was built ...

   a) ☐ more than hundred years ago.

   b) ☐ in the 21st century.

   c) ☐ in 1974.

2 The European rulers came from different European countries. Name <u>one</u>.

_____

3 Over one million people in South Africa ...

   a) ☐ are Muslim.

   b) ☐ are Asian.

   c) ☐ are from Bo-Kaap.

4 What sort of work did Asian workers do outside of Cape Town?

   a) _____

   b) _____

5 The Bo-Kaap Museum ...

   a) ☐ was built in 1964.

   b) ☐ has exhibitions but no furniture.

   c) ☐ gives information about the Asian population of Cape Town.

6 In Bo Kaap, you can even see Asian culture, because the houses on Wale Street are ...

_____.

2. Hörverstehen – Teil 2

A presentation about William Shakespeare

Amina and Mason are giving a presentation about William Shakespeare.

- *First read the tasks 1–6.*
- *Then listen to the presentation.*
- *While you are listening, tick the correct box, answer the question, match the sentence halves or fill in the information.*
- *At the end you will hear the presentation again.*
- *Now read the tasks 1–6. You have* **one minute** *to do this.*

🎧
10

- *Now listen to the guide and do the tasks.*

William Shakespeare (1564–1616)

1 Shakespeare wrote his plays many years ago, ...

   a) ☐ so his plays are mostly read, but not performed today.

   b) ☐ but you can still see his plays in many theatres today.

   c) ☐ so today you can only see them in Britain.

2 Not much is known about Shakespeare's private life. But we know that he ...

   a) ☐ was born and died in London. **b)** ☐ married at the age of 20.

   c) ☐ had two daughters and a son.

3 Something terrible happened to one of William Shakespeare's family members. What was it?

   _____

4 Match each of the place names (1–3) with one of the explanations (A–D).
   You will <u>not need one</u> explanation.

	A is where Shakespeare **went to school**.
1 The house in Henley Street ...	B is where Shakespeare **was born**.
2 Mary Arden's farm ...	C is where Shakespeare's **father worked**.
3 Old Town Hall ...	D was **owned by** Shakespeare's **mother**.

5 What is special about the old buildings from Shakespeare's time? Give **two** examples.

   _____

   _____

6 The Globe Theatre in London today ...

   a) ☐ is the same old theatre where Shakespeare worked.

   b) ☐ is a modern copy of the theatre from Shakespeare's days.

   c) ☐ is not like the theatre Shakespeare used.

Zweiter Prüfungsteil:
Leseverstehen – Wortschatz – Schreiben

3. Leseverstehen

High-rise living in Britain

The following text is from the lifestyle section of a British newspaper.

> • First read the text.
> • Then do the tasks 1–6. Decide if the statements are true or false, tick the correct boxes and give evidence. You <u>can</u> quote from the text.

Tower block in London

Say the words "high-rise apartment blocks" in Britain and people think of the very first tower blocks built in the 1960s for people in lower-paid jobs. The flats were small and the entrances were dark and dirty, full of rubbish and graffiti. The lifts kept breaking down. That was no joke if you lived on the 10th floor and arrived home with your week's shopping or a child in a wheelchair. The general opinion was that people only lived in such buildings if they had no alternative.

Of course, the tower blocks have always had their fans, because of the amazing views from the higher flats. People living in tower blocks also often say that they feel safer than in a house. After all, nobody can climb through the window of a flat on the 16th floor. In fact, nobody can even look in. And there are almost no mice, ants and spiders in the flats.

In the past, most people didn't like apartment blocks. But things have changed. Look at the skyline of most British cities today and you'll see that apartment blocks are going up all around you. So why have flats become so popular? One reason is that prices for land have gone up, so houses are becoming more and more expensive – too expensive for many families. Building taller, it seems, is the only way of building cheaper homes.

It is true that families with children still like to live in a house with a front door, a back door and a garden. But these days people who live on their own or childless couples often get home from work late and have no time for garden work. Instead, they prefer to have a few plants on an easily-managed balcony. That's why the apartments going up today are built to attract people with well-paying jobs. The new flats are large and airy. CCTV cameras keep the entrances safe, and companies clean the corridors and repair the lifts.

What's more, we now know that high-rise apartment blocks are healthier than you think. Experts from the University of Bern in Switzerland found that people who live on the 8th floor or above have a good chance of living longer than those who live on the lower floors. Those living higher up, they say, don't die of lung or heart illnesses as often as people on lower floors. That's because walking up more stairs keeps people healthier and they live longer. The air is also cleaner on the higher floors and people hear less of the traffic noise.

The British population will grow from about 65 million in 2016 to 75 million by 2040. So there will be a need for millions of new homes. If we want to protect our environment, we will have to build homes in our cities. But we all know that land in cities is expensive, too expensive for millions of new houses. It is clear, then, that in the future more people will have to live in flats. The apartment blocks being built today are here to stay.

1 The flats in the 1960s tower blocks were ...

a) ☐ not clean, but had good lifts instead of stairs.

b) ☐ ideal for families with disabled children.

c) ☐ often in poor condition.

2 Some people don't want to live in houses because they're afraid of people breaking into their homes.

This statement is ...   ☐ true.   ☐ false.

One piece of evidence from the text: _____

_____

3 One advantage of flats <u>described in the text</u> is that ...

a) ☐ they don't have a garden.

b) ☐ there are fewer insects or other small animals than in houses.

c) ☐ the walls are thicker, so you don't hear the neighbours.

One piece of evidence from the text: _____

_____

4 A lot of families want to live in high-rise apartment blocks.

This statement is ...   ☐ true.   ☐ false.

One piece of evidence from the text: _____

_____

5 According to experts, living on higher floors in apartment blocks ...

a) ☐ is unhealthy.

b) ☐ helps people become older.

c) ☐ is dangerous because the air is dirtier.

6 The writer is concerned about the nature around the cities.

This statement is ...   ☐ true.   ☐ false.

One piece of evidence from the text: _____

_____

4. Wortschatz

The joys of travelling

Yolanda from Poland loves travelling. She gives some of her reasons in an article for an online magazine.

4.1 Part 1

- *Complete the sentences 1–6 with words from the box.*
- *Use each word only <u>once</u>.*
- *There is <u>one more word</u> than you need.*

annoyed	bored	solve	deal	frustrating	station	alternative

I really think that travelling helps you become a better person. I'll tell you why.

1   Travelling helps you to be more flexible and confident because you learn to

_____ with unexpected problems.

2   For example you may have to decide what to do if you arrive at the _____

and find out that you have missed your train.

3   Or you may have to make _____ plans if you wanted to be lazy and lie on

the beach all day, but you can't because it's raining.

4   Having to change plans can be really _____ .

5   Your first reaction is to be _____ because you can't do what you wanted

to do.

6   But so often when you travel you meet people who can help you _____

your problems. You start chatting, you share a joke, and you feel much better.

4.2 Part 2

> - *Complete the sentences 1–6 with <u>suitable</u> words.*
> - *Give only <u>one</u> solution.*

1   But you will learn that these _____ almost always lead to new, positive

    experiences. In fact, this is how you make many new friends.

2   And these moments make the best memories. Keep a diary, so you will never

    _____ them!

3   Another good thing about travelling is that you _____ things about other

    countries that you cannot learn from books.

4   Discovering _____ cultures, food and lifestyles will make you think about

    your own life.

5   And maybe you'll learn new things, like using a _____ instead of your

    smartphone to find your way around.

6   And finally, you will really _____ sleeping in your own bed after travelling

    for a while. That will make it easier for you when you return home at the end of your journey.

5. Schreiben

Ben is your email partner from Scotland. You already exchanged a few emails.

- Read Ben's email and write back to him.
- Answer <u>all</u> of his questions.
- Remember to write <u>complete sentences</u> and include a nice beginning and a friendly ending.
- Write about **120 words**.

Hi!

Thank you for your letter and sorry for my late answer! I'm very busy at the moment.
I hope your are doing fine. I am very well myself.

Recently I started working as a server at a cafe in my town. It is a lot of fun. Sometimes I help in the kitchen, but most of the time I am serving customers, making coffee and preparing sandwiches. And my colleagues are great, too.
Unfortunately, I often have to work on the weekends. Also, serving means that I have to stand and walk a lot. But on the other hand, I was able to buy a new smartphone using the money I earned.

What about you?
Did you already have a job? Or are you planning on starting one?
What job would you like to do and why?
Tell me about the skills you need for the job!
Is there anything you hate in a job? Why?
I am very much looking forward to your next letter.
Take care,
Ben

Erster Prüfungsteil: Hörverstehen

1. Hörverstehen – Teil 1

Tourist attractions in Brighton

You will hear two reporters talking about two popular tourist attractions in Brighton, a city on the southern coast of Britain.

> • *First read the tasks 1–6.*
> • *Then listen to the programme.*
> • *While you are listening, tick the correct box, answer the question or fill in the information.*
> • *At the end you will hear the guide again.*
> • *Now read the tasks 1–6. You have **one minute** to do this.*

The British Airways i360 in Brighton

🎧
11

> • *Now listen to the guide and do the tasks.*

1 In Brighton …

    a) ☐ the weather is always great.

    b) ☐ it is always raining.

    c) ☐ it is not often warm enough to go swimming.

2 The British Airways i360 is a high concrete tower. Say <u>how high</u> it is.

_____

3 The tickets for the rides are more _____ for tourists.

4 Where does the dirty water in the tunnels of the Brighton sewers come from? Name two places.

_____

_____

5 The sewers were built because

    a) ☐ other cities built them, too.

    b) ☐ the dirty water in the streets smelled really bad.

    c) ☐ they prevent people from getting sick.

6 <u>How old</u> do you have to be to visit the Brighton sewers?

_____

2. Hörverstehen – Teil 2

Cricket in India

Aarav Malhotra is a radio reporter in Delhi.
You are going to hear a radio interview about the sport cricket and India's role in this sport.

> • *First read the tasks 1 – 6.*
> • *Then listen to the interview.*
> • *While you are listening, tick the correct box or fill in the information.*
> • *At the end you will hear the interview again.*
> • *Now read the tasks 1 – 6. You have **one minute** to do this.*

> • *Now listen to the interview and do the tasks.*

Cricket is a popular sport in many parts of the world

1   Aarav Malhotra asks which two sports ...

   a) ☐ have the most players

   b) ☐ are played in most countries

   c) ☐ have the most fans

in the world.

2   The number of countries in the Cricket World Cup ...

   a) ☐ was low in 1975 and is now higher.

   b) ☐ was high in 1975 and is now lower.

   c) ☐ is bigger than in the Basketball World Cup.

3   India ...

   a) ☐ has never won the Cricket World Cup.

   b) ☐ is more successful in cricket than Australia.

   c) ☐ is less successful in cricket than Australia.

4   The cricket players who earn the most money ...

   a) ☐ are Indian and play in Indian teams.

   b) ☐ are Europeans and Americans who play in India.

   c) ☐ once played for India, but not any more.

5   According to Aarav, people in countries that don't play cricket ...

   a) ☐ think that cricket is not a real sport.

   b) ☐ think that cricket is a modern sport.

   c) ☐ are familiar with the rules of the game.

6   Cricket has changed in the last few years. How? Give **one** example.

Zweiter Prüfungsteil:
Leseverstehen – Wortschatz – Schreiben

3. Leseverstehen

Stereotypically Irish?

This article is from a British magazine.

- First read the text.
- Then do the tasks 1–6.
- For tasks 1 and 3, decide if the statements are true or false and give evidence. You can quote from the text.
- For tasks 2, 4, 5 and 6 choose the correct answer.

Ireland's famous Cliffs of Moher

There are lots of stereotypes for different countries around the world. People often think of Lederhosen, sausage and beer for Germany. But what about Ireland? When you hear "Irish
5 stereotypes", what typically comes to mind? Red-haired, potato-eating, Guinness-drinking Catholics with large families? It turns out that these stereotypes are not helpful at all if you want to know who the Irish are today.

10 Red hair is in fact more common in Ireland than it is worldwide. A lot of people in Ireland have red hair – around 10 %. That's about 420,000 people. However, there are many, many more redheads in the U.S., somewhere between
15 six to eighteen million people! The Udmurt people from the Volga region in Russia also have a high percentage of redheaded people, similar to Ireland. But there are not as many Udmurt people, so there are also not as many Udmurt
20 redheads.

The stereotypically Irish meal is meat and potatoes. But that is absolutely not true! Ireland is making a name for itself in the food world. Chefs in Irish restaurants are modernising
25 traditional dishes by mixing fresh local products with exciting ingredients and flavours from all over the world.

And please be careful with this next stereotype though, it can be very offensive to Irish
30 people: the stereotype that Irish love alcohol. Pubs are an important part of Irish culture, but they offer more than just alcohol. People also go there to have a family meal or to meet friends. In fact, 1/5 of the adult Irish population say that
35 they do not drink any alcohol at all. The problem

is, while not all Irish people drink, those who do, drink way too much. But "mindful drinking" is becoming trendier, and non-alcoholic drinks are more popular than ever.

40 Ireland is often seen as a conservative country, made up of Catholic people who are very religious, and who think tradition is extremely important. But fewer and fewer people are going to church services on a regular
45 basis. One reason for this change is that, since the 1990s, many reports of sexual abuse by Catholic priests have come out. These horrible scandals shocked the whole country. Before these reports came out, the church had had a lot more influence on Irish society.

50 Large families may have been common in the past, but today just 1.4 children per family are the average in Ireland, lower than the average 2.3 children in the EU overall. But just like the rest of Europe, people are living together
55 before getting married and getting married later in life. They are having children later in life and having fewer children overall. Ireland has a lower divorce rate compared with the rest of the EU. Ireland today also has more single-parent
60 families, more same-sex partnerships, and more families with mixed-nationalities and migrant backgrounds than the EU average.

So, if most of these stereotypes turn out to be wrong, why do we continue to believe them,
65 or at the very least, joke about them? Ireland is a modern, diverse country and cannot be generalised! Ideally, you should go and find out for yourself what makes Ireland "Irish".

1 The writer is surprised at how useful stereotypes can be.

This statement is ... ☐ true. ☐ false.

One piece of evidence from the text: _____

_____

2 There are more redheads ...

a) ☐ in Ireland than in the U.S.

b) ☐ in Russia than in Ireland.

c) ☐ in the U.S. than in Ireland.

3 Irish meals still only include ingredients from Ireland.

This statement is ... ☐ true. ☐ false.

One piece of evidence from the text: _____

_____

4 Pubs in Ireland ...

a) ☐ are not very popular.

b) ☐ offer drinks, but no food.

c) ☐ are family places, too.

5 In Ireland, the number of people attending church services ...

a) ☐ is going up.

b) ☐ is staying the same.

c) ☐ is going down.

6 Couples in Ireland ...

a) ☐ are getting married earlier in life

b) ☐ are getting divorced less frequently

c) ☐ are having more children

... than the EU average.

4. Wortschatz

How shopping has changed

Simon writes a blog. Today he is writing about how shopping used to be very different for his family in the past. Read his blog.

4.1 Part 1

> • *Complete the following text (sentences 1–6)*
>   *with* <u>suitable</u> *words.*
> • *Give only* <u>one</u> *solution.*

1   In my great grandparents' generation, it was the wife who went shopping while her

    _____ went to work. And in the evening she made dinner for him.

2   At first, shopping meant going from shop to shop to buy different things. My great grandmother

    went to the baker's for bread, to the greengrocer's for fruit and vegetables, and to the butcher's for

    _____ like steak, ham and sausages.

3   My great grandmother said what she wanted, and each shopkeeper _____

    her by picking the items off a shelf.

4   Of course, this all took a long time, so _____ stood in a line and chatted

    with the people in front or behind them.

5   However, in the 1960s, supermarkets began to appear, and my great grandmother got used to

    putting her _____ into a shopping basket herself.

6   At the checkout she got lots of plastic bags to _____ her shopping home.

4.2 Part 2

- *Complete the following text with words from the box.*
- *Use each word only <u>once</u>.*
- *You <u>won't need one</u> of the words.*

result	floors	search	expensive	environment	instead	growth

1   Back then nobody worried about all those plastic bags. Nobody talked about pollution and the

   problems this creates for our whole _____.

2   In the late 1970s, shopping changed again. Supermarkets got bigger and bigger, and customers like

   my grandparents got used to paying by credit card _____ of cash.

3   By introducing shopping centres, the shopping experience was made as easy as possible. Inside

   these department stores, there were lifts and escalators to move customers up to the

   upper _____.

4   Recently, with the rapid _____ of online shopping, the way we shop has

   changed again.

5   Without even leaving their homes, customers simply _____ the

   supermarkets' websites, click on the items they need and pay online.

6   One _____ of online shopping is that some shopping centres are

   disappearing. There will certainly be other changes too, but it is still too early to predict them.

5. Schreiben

You are planning to work abroad after leaving school. On the Internet you have found the following two job adverts.

- *Read the job advertisements.*
- *Choose one job you want to apply for.*

Come work at Trifdon Castle!	**The Pennymoore Day Centre is looking for assistant helpers!**
• Are you looking for an exciting and challenging summer job? • Would you like to live in a castle for the summer? • Do you speak some English and at least one other language? We are offering a summer job in the souvenir shop in the famous Trifdon Castle. Come and help us with our many visitors from all over the world. ***It's a great chance to improve your English! Free accommodation.*** Please send your application by email to: trifdoncastle@example.com	We need young people to … • serve tea and snacks, • chat with the old people staying with us, • help the elderly with their shopping. We can offer you … • a good pay, • accommodation next to a park and a swimming pool. ***Would you like to join our team?*** Just contact: pennymooredc@example.net

Write an email application.
Include the following information:
- *personal details*
- *general interests*
- *your motivation for the job you chose*
- *your qualifications*

*Write about **120 words**.*
Remember the formal characteristics of a letter of application.

Erster Prüfungsteil: Hörverstehen

1. Hörverstehen – Teil 1

The D of E expedition

You are going to hear an interview with two young hikers on an adventure trip.

> * *First read the tasks 1–6.*
> * *Then listen to the interview.*
> * *While you are listening, answer the questions, tick the correct box, match the statements, and fill in the gaps.*
> * *At the end you will hear the interview again.*
> * *Now read the tasks 1–6. You have one minute to do this.*

> * *Now listen to the story and do the tasks.*

1 Why did Jack sleep badly?

_____

2 The reporter is surprised because Katie ...

a) ☐ has muddy feet.

b) ☐ is missing one of her shoes.

c) ☐ looks stupid.

3 The aim of the *D of E Award* is to make young people experience _____ in the outdoors.

4 Make **two** true sentences.

On the silver level ...	A you are on an expedition for three days and two nights.
	B you don't need any equipment.
	C you need more to eat and to wear than on the bronze level.
	D you carry more camping equipment than on the bronze level.

5 Smartphones are allowed ...

a) ☐ to call for help.

b) ☐ to navigate.

c) ☐ to get messages.

6 What happened when Jack and Katie didn't find their way?

_____

2. Hörverstehen – Teil 2

A presentation about Wales

Four students in a school in Baltimore, USA, are giving a presentation about Wales.

> • First read the tasks 1–6.
> • Then listen to the presentation.
> • While you are listening, tick the correct box, say if the statements are true or false, answer the questions and fill in the information.
> • At the end you will hear the presentation again.
> • Now read the tasks 1–6. You have <u>one minute</u> to do this.

14

> • Now listen to the presentation and do the tasks.

1 In the EURO 2016 Football Championship Wales ...

a) ☐ won against England.

b) ☐ played better than England.

c) ☐ did not have an own team.

2 What do people from Wales answer when they are asked about their nationality?

_____

3 The Welsh language is ...

a) ☐ a dialect of English.

b) ☐ mostly like English.

c) ☐ not like English at all.

4 You immediately notice that people speak two languages in Wales because of the bilingual

_____ .

5 In the centre of Wales you'll find ...

a) ☐ lots of farm animals.

b) ☐ mountains that are smaller than those in Enland.

c) ☐ the larger towns of Wales.

6 Most of the castles in Wales were ...

a) ☐ built by a Welsh king to protect Wales from the English.

b) ☐ built by an English king.

c) ☐ completely destroyed.

Zweiter Prüfungsteil:
Leseverstehen – Wortschatz – Schreiben

3. Leseverstehen

Good health in Australia?

This article is from a British fitness and health magazine.

> - *First read the text.*
> - *Then do the tasks 1–6. Tick the correct box, give quotes as evidence from the text and match the statements.*

For many people, sport, health and Australia go together like bread, butter and jam. Australians are stars in cricket, rugby, tennis and sailing. Per inhabitant, Australia won more
5 medals in the last two summer Olympics than Britain, Germany or the USA. All the people smiling at you from Australian travel brochures or TV screens are beautiful and healthy. And not only in the adverts. In TV shows the lifeguards
10 who save people from dying in swimming accidents are all young, healthy and athletic, too.

No wonder Australia is so popular with emigrants from Europe. Over 200,000 Brits emigrated to Australia between 2010 and 2015.
15 That's three times the number that went to live in the USA. And the stories of sunshine, barbecues and beach volleyball these British emigrants tell contrast with our life indoors in the UK. The Australian sun, we think, helps
20 Australians to keep fit and healthy. Our rainy weather gives us a good excuse to watch TV, and eat and drink too much.

But reality is different. Australia's sunshine can be a killer because it causes skin cancer. For
25 many years Australia had the highest number of deadly skin cancers in the world: 49 out of every 100,000 Australians suffered from this dangerous illness in 2005. Health experts now expect this number to fall to 41 in the next
30 fifteen years. The reason for this is that Australians have learned to use suncream and hats. But even this lower number is still two or three times higher than in the UK.

The high rate of skin cancers is maybe not
35 unusual in a country with hot sunshine, but another health problem may be a surprise:

Australians carry many more kilos than people in France or Germany. In 2007, 67 % of Australian adults are overweight. This was the third highest number in the English-speaking world after the
40 USA and New Zealand. And the problem is growing faster in Australia than anywhere else in the world. On average, Australians are now as heavy as people in the USA.

Why the problem with the extra kilos?
45 There are two reasons. One is that Australians don't eat enough fruit and vegetables. Almost half of all Australians eat enough fruit every day, but only 7 % eat enough vegetables. More and more Australians are buying unhealthy
50 food from fast-food restaurants. The second reason is that too few Australians do enough sport. Just over half of all Australians do 150 minutes of sport activity per week. But just under half do not. Almost 15 % do no sport
55 activity at all.

Australia is of course not alone with this problem. And no country in the world has yet found an answer to it. However, the problems of skin cancer and extra kilos contrast with
60 Australia's image of fitness and health. In future, it will be more difficult to find athletic looking Australians for the photos in holiday brochures.

1   In TV shows, the lifeguards are often overweight.

This statement is ...   ☐ true.   ☐ false.

One piece of evidence from the text: _____

_____

2   When British emigrants talk about their life in Australia, they ...

a) ☐ say that they sit at home and put on weight.

b) ☐ give a positive picture of Australia.

c) ☐ say that they liked the UK better.

3   Make **two** true sentences.

Because of the sun ...	A	people needed to start wearing sun protection.
	B	Australians are mostly staying indoors.
	C	a high number of Australians got skin cancer.

4   There are more overweight people in Australia than in the US.

This statement is ...   ☐ true.   ☐ false.

One piece of evidence from the text: _____

_____

5   One of the problems is that most Australians ...

a) ☐ do not get enough exercise.

b) ☐ eat too much meat.

c) ☐ eat too many sweet fruits.

6   The image of Australia in brochures and TV series is false.

This statement is ...   ☐ true.   ☐ false.

One piece of evidence from the text: _____

_____

4. Wortschatz

Life in the Outback

Noah's parents are farmers in the Australian Outback. He describes life in the Outback for an online magazine.

4.1 Part 1

> *Complete the sentences 1– 6 by ticking the correct box.*

1 Most Australians live in large cities. Sydney, for example, is a city with a

   a) ☐ people b) ☐ population c) ☐ migration d) ☐ pollution

   of 5.25 million inhabitants.

2 The lifestyle in Sydney is in many ways ...

   a) ☐ likely b) ☐ similar c) ☐ other d) ☐ reasonable

   to that of people living in any large cities anywhere in the world.

3 People in Sydney also have problems in the morning traffic and spend the day working in an office

   a) ☐ housing. b) ☐ home. c) ☐ apartment. d) ☐ building.

4 Life is very different for the minority of Australians who live in the Outback. There are no traffic jams here. In fact there often aren't

   a) ☐ even b) ☐ ever c) ☐ every d) ☐ very

   roads. Most people drive the last few miles home on small dirt paths.

5 During the rainy season many of these dirt paths are ...

   a) ☐ bottled b) ☐ bored c) ☐ blocked d) ☐ borrowed

   because they are so muddy.

6 The ...

   a) ☐ consequence b) ☐ connection c) ☐ comparison d) ☐ competence

   is that people have to buy everything they need well in advance and store things in huge storage rooms and refrigerators.

4.2 Part 2

- *Complete the sentences 1–6 with <u>suitable</u> words.*
- *Give only <u>one</u> solution per gap.*

1 The dry season in the Outback, on the other _____, means no

   rain at all for weeks.

2 In these times of dryness there is a serious lack of _____, and farmers in

   the Outback have to work extra hard to care for their plants and animals.

3 Farmers often live miles away from their nearest neighbours, so they have to be clever and tough.

   They need to be able to solve _____ on their own.

4 Primary and secondary schools can be far away, so the biggest problem for

   _____ in the Outback is their education.

5 Children do lots of their lessons online. So they mostly work and play on their own. And they often

   feel _____ because they have so little contact with other children.

6 That's why barbecues and festivals are an _____ part of life in the Outback.

   They offer the chance to meet other people, to have fun together and to make new friends.

5. Schreiben

You ordered a new tablet from a British online shop. Unfortunately, there were some problems.

Write a <u>letter of complaint</u> to send to their customer service.

Include the following aspects:
- The tablet arrived three weeks later than expected.
- The box around the tablet was broken.
- There was a scratch on the display.
- There was no charger included.
- You want the company to replace the tablet.

Remember to include a friendly beginning and a nice ending.
Write about **120 words**.

Übersicht über die Aufgaben zum Hörverstehen

Die Tonaufnahmen (MP3-Dateien) und die Hörtexte findest du online unter www.scook.de.
Deinen persönlichen Zugangscode findest du auf Seite 1 deines Abschlussprüfungstrainers.

Track	Kapitel	Titel	Seite
1	Training Section	Calgary's skyways (Part 1)	8
2	Training Section	Calgary's skyways (Part 2)	9
3	Training Section	Calgary's skyways (Part 3)	9
4	Training Section	Calgary's skyways (Part 4)	10
5	Training Section	The Niagara Falls (Version 1)	10
6	Training Section	The Niagara Falls (Version 2)	11
7	Training Section	The *Tour de Yorkshire*	13
8	Training Section	Bob Marley	14
9	Musterprüfung 1	Bo-Kaap – a special district in Cape Town	42
10	Musterprüfung 1	A presentation about William Shakespeare	43
11	Musterprüfung 2	Tourist attractions in Brighton	49
12	Musterprüfung 2	Cricket in India	50
13	Musterprüfung 3	The *D of E* expedition	56
14	Musterprüfung 3	A presentation about Wales	57
15	Urheberrechtserklärung		

Studio: Clarity Studio Berlin

Regie und Aufnahmeleitung: Christian Schmitz

Tontechnik: Huseyin Dönertaş, Christian Marx, Pascal Thinius

Illustrationen

Karen Donnelly: **S. 9**, **S. 18**

Fotos

S. 9: Shutterstock.com/Jeff Whyte; **S. 10**: Shutterstock.com/Mikhail Kolesnikov; **S. 13**: Shutterstock.com/ Constantin Stanciu; **S. 14**: interfoto e.k./Friedrich; **S. 16**: mauritius images/alamy stock photo/Penny Tweedie; **S. 17**: Shutterstock.com/Tukaram.Karve; **S. 19**: Shutterstock.com/Photomika-com; **S. 21**: Shutterstock.com/Boyloso; **S. 22**: Shutterstock.com/Evocation Images; **S. 23**: Shutterstock.com/mubus7; **S. 26**: Shutterstock.com/wavebreakmedia; **S. 28**: imago stock&people/Panthermedia; **S. 36**: Shutterstock.com/ anon_tae; **S. 38** li.: Shutterstock.com/VisionPro; re.: Shutterstock.com/Tropical studio; **S. 42**: Shutterstock. com/David Pickett; **S. 43**: akg-images/Fototeca Gilardi; **S. 44**: Shutterstock.com/Dragan Jovanovic; **S. 49**: Shutterstock.com/Jevanto Productions; **S. 50**: Shutterstock.com/imagedb.com; **S. 51**: Shutterstock.com/ Patryk Kosmider; **S. 53**: interfoto e.k./SuperStock; **S. 56**: Shutterstock.com/Oleksandr Nagaiets; **S. 57**: Shutterstock.com/Katariina Järvinen; **S. 58**: Shutterstock.com/Rawpixel.com; **S. 60**: Shutterstock.com/ Bernd Leitner Fotodesign.